Liberated is a thoroughly bib subject and brings a heady blenc candor. By exposing the serious Luther, not to mention the blind spots of the wider Christian church, and in dealing with some of the most shocking abuses of women in scripture, Karen inspires confidence that she will be honest in her handling of the Biblical text. This is an important apologetic that the church needs to read and reflect upon carefully, if we are to convince a watching world that ultimate dignity and flourishing is to be found in following Jesus of Nazareth.

Richard Cunningham
Director, Universities and Colleges Christian Fellowship
(UCCF), United Kingdom

I am so grateful for this book. Karen Soole compellingly presents the Bible's exalted view of women. She also tackles some of those passages in the Bible which many find most challenging. Reading it will fill both women and men with confidence in what it means to be a truly liberated woman in the 21st century.

William Taylor
Minister of St. Helen's Bishopsgate, London

What are we to do when the world says the Bible's view of women is utterly abhorrent, and consigning them to a life of domesticity is totally demeaning? What are we to do when the Bible affirms the leadership of men and appears to devalue women, treating them as second-class and even 'abusable' citizens? Answer: read the Bible again. Karen Soole rightly challenges these assumptions as either completely false or only teaching what is partially true – which, in the end, is just as damaging. She helpfully shows how women have always played an equally important role in fulfilling God's purposes (think of Tamar, Hannah and Abigail) and when they are devalued and mistreated, God's justice in condemning the abusers and vindicating the abused is undeniable.

Drawing on her extensive knowledge of English literature and modern culture, Karen challenges the way women have been portrayed throughout history and sets the record straight. Not many Christian writers can quote Shakespeare, Jane Austen, Simone de Beauvoir, Germaine Greer, Phoebe Waller-Bridge and Taylor Swift like she can, while, at the same time, showing how the Bible exposes their weaknesses and false suppositions. But this book is not a feminist tirade against men – far from it. Karen shows us again and again that God values men and women equally and gives them both the task of being His image bearers in the world. And Christ Himself, the supreme image of the invisible God, is the one we should look to, because ultimate liberation is found in Him alone. This book will help Christian men and women to stop feeling suspicious or threatened by one another, and shows that bearing God's image in a Christ-like way is the secret to human flourishing.

Carrie Sandom

Director of Women's Ministry at The Proclamation Trust, London

I wish this book had been around when I was first a Christian, wondering whether a fiercely independent, single, domestically-challenged woman like me could thrive in a faith that some claim oppresses women. Soole's compelling writing, cultural insights and biblical wisdom show how God honours women far more than our contemporary culture does. Tracing the rich scriptural narrative from Creation to New Creation, Soole demonstrates that God's purposes have always been to dignify and equally value women in all their diverse skills and roles. Essential reading for both women and men.

Anne Witton
Content Director at Living Out

There are plenty of places in which women are undervalued, demeaned or treated as second-class citizens. Karen Soole convincingly removes the Bible from the company of the misogynists at the local golf club, big business board members and internet trolls. Even better, she shows how the Bible's message contains better news for women than that coming from any other source. I hope both women and men will read and discover that the living God truly is a friend of women.

Peter Dray
Director of Creative Evangelism, Universities and Colleges
Christian Fellowship (UCCF), United Kingdom

LIBERATED

HOW THE BIBLE EXALTS AND DIGNIFIES WOMEN

KAREN SOOLE

CHRISTIAN
FOCUS

Copyright © Karen Soole 2021

paperback ISBN 978-1-5271-0729-8
ebook ISBN 978-1-5271-0852-3

10 9 8 7 6 5 4 3 2 1

Published in 2021
by
Christian Focus Publications, Ltd.
Geanies House, Fearn,
Ross-shire, IV20 1TW, Scotland.
www.christianfocus.com

Cover design by Tom Barnard

Printed and bound by
Bell & Bain, Glasgow

CONTENTS

To Lizzie, Polly, George and Max.

Thank you all for your questions and for never being happy with glib answers. Keep asking, keep searching, God longs to make Himself known.

ACKNOWLEDGEMENTS

This book has been born out of numerous conversations, some who patiently helped me as I searched the Scriptures and others who challenged my understanding as they too grappled to understand. They know who they are.

I want to thank, in particular, the women who came with their questions and were not happy to settle with easy answers. Your encouragement persuaded me to write this book for the many others who are just like you.

Thank you to my church family at Trinity Church Lancaster for all your prayers and support.

Thank you to my husband, Martin. He has championed my ministry and urged me to continue with this project. I owe so much to him, I cannot begin to say ...

Thank you to our Lord Jesus Christ, who has held me through my doubts, questions and struggles and continues to lead me into the riches of His grace.

INTRODUCTION

A young woman exploring the Christian faith visited a church and was struck by the absence of women's voices during the service. She decided to enquire about it afterwards, so she approached one of the male leaders and asked: 'What do the women do?' He replied without a flicker of hesitation: 'They make the coffee'. This man's casual acceptance of women's domestic role left her cold. Could it be that God restricts women in this way? It reinforced her suspicion that the Bible offers women less than men and is the enemy of equality.

A generation that knows independence and is striving for self-determination is highly suspicious of Christianity. Equality for all people is a foundational principle in our culture and embedded in our law. There are debates over whether or not we should aim for equality of outcome or equality of opportunity, but the consensus is clear: all people are equally valuable. However, religion is seen as a stronghold that promotes inequality. There is a widespread belief that the Bible is sexist. Women, in particular, can fear that God does not want their good and instead, He wants to box them in and clip their wings. Our culture believes that they need to forget religion to achieve equality. Elizabeth Cady Stanton, one of the early American suffragists, said:

> *Whatever the Bible may be made to do in Hebrew or Greek, in plain English it does not exalt and dignify women.*[1]

It's a serious charge against a text that sets out to do the exact opposite. The principle of equality is established in the first pages of the Bible, and its message does exalt and dignify both men and women. However, I understand the sense of unease that some have when they read the Bible. There are parts of the Bible that I have struggled with, and bits that seemed far removed from my life as a twenty-first-century woman. I have wrestled with them, but as I read, I came to know that God offers more liberation, more freedom, and more fulfilment than I could dare to imagine. His Word has made sense to me in a way no other philosophy or perspective ever has. God's Word has given me clarity and enabled me to stand securely despite our broken world. I have discovered that Jesus is the way, the truth, and the life.

Elizabeth Cady Stanton was convinced that the Bible was not about liberation but bondage. Is it possible that she misread the Bible? In her treatise against the Bible, she threw down this gauntlet:

---

1   Elizabeth Cady Stanton, *The Woman's Bible* (1895), (Pacific Publishing Studio, 2010), p. x

To women still believing in the plenary inspiration of the scriptures, we say give us, by all means, your exegesis....[2]

In this book, I am taking up her challenge. I want to share with you what I have discovered as I read the Bible and grappled with it over many years. You will notice that I do not directly address the differences in church practice concerning women's ministry. This is deliberate. It is a subject that is covered in great detail elsewhere. My aim is for this book to address the fear that God does not exalt or dignify women. Before we can begin to consider church practice, we need to know that we can trust that God is good. Only then can we ask what it means for women to serve Him.

I invite you to come with me on my journey. It will take us through the Bible story from Genesis to Revelation so you can decide whether God is offering life and liberation, or suffocation and oppression. I want to invite you to meet the God of the Bible. It is common to misread strangers, but when we take time to get to know someone, we discover that our preconceptions were mistaken. I would love for you to take some time out to get to know God and check out for yourself whether He is trustworthy or not.

Don't dismiss this book as 'for women only'. These things matter to everyone. I have written this for men and women, but I will be addressing concerns that women face in particular. I am convinced, however, that these concerns are relevant to everyone. At the end of each chapter, there are questions for you to mull over. You can do these on your own, but it may

---

2   Ibid., p. ix

be more fun to discuss them in a book group or with a friend who is reading the book too. Why not read a chapter a week and then meet up for a coffee (insert drink of choice here) and look at the questions together? The questions are designed for beginning a conversation and for helping you answer the question – does God offer me liberation or oppression? Can I trust that God is good?

1 THIRSTY

One of my earliest memories is of re-enacting the adventures of Marine Boy – the first Japanese Manga to be shown on British television. I was not more than three but knew that the 'best' character was Marine Boy and not Neptina, his friend the mermaid. I had no interest in the girl's part. Growing up in the 1970s, I thought that it was rubbish to be a girl. I was unaware of the women's liberation movement exploding around me; instead, I was dealing with my own frustrations. One was the separation of the sexes at playtime in my primary school. I was banished to a world of girls playing 'horses', skipping and doing handstands except I didn't know their skipping games and never mastered the art of the handstand. My pockets were full of conkers and marbles and no one to play them with. As the youngest with three older brothers, I learnt to fight my corner, I proudly called myself a tomboy and looked down on 'girly' girls. Out of school, my friends were all boys, we clambered over seaside rocks, rode our bikes, made dens and caught crabs. I found girls more difficult; they were always falling out and not talking to each other. Boys could be troublesome too: I broke my collarbone being made to walk the plank while playing pirates. I was frequently tied up as a prisoner in the shed and was always on the losing end of fights with my brothers, but that aside, I loved them. Before adolescence kicked in, I definitely wanted to be a boy.

Church did not help in this. The women all wore terrible clothes, Sunday best complete with hats and gloves – yes I am really that old! My mother, who had longed for a girl after three boys, dressed me up in Crimplene frocks with knee-high white socks and buckle shoes that I hated. I was so grateful when she finally made me a 1970s trouser suit that was considered smart enough for church. But my biggest hate was reserved for the Girls' Brigade. Their uniform was a red polo neck top under a navy pinafore dress, white tights and polished black shoes. We were crowned with a flat hat held on by elastic under our chins. Once a month it was parade Sunday and once a month I had to wear this attire to church. This was not the worst part. My brothers, as members of the Boys' Brigade, were all encouraged to play in a brass band. They each chose an instrument, a trumpet, a bugle and drums and led the parade around the town while we walked behind them. We girls did nothing but follow; there were no instruments for us. This was the ultimate humiliation.

I grew up and discovered that life throws much tougher obstacles at people. I began to enjoy being a woman, although I struggled to shake off the sense that somehow I was an imposter and not appropriately feminine or skilled in things that mattered, like cooking. My sense of womanhood was negative. I saw women as less important than men, even though I was living at the time of Britain's first female prime minister. Where did my negativity come from? Was it the church, or was it the general culture of 1970s Margate? I grew up in the church, and the church I attended had no female role models to aspire to. My secondary school was a Girls' Grammar School, but it did not help us with our aspirations, and we were directed to be secretaries, nurses or mothers. I had one history teacher whose ultimate exasperated criticism was, 'You are the sort of girl who drinks out of a mug!' Drinking from mugs being the norm at home, I never understood why they were a problem. I did learn that being a girl meant pleasing men and being quiet. It does not take long for this attitude to lead you to believe your significance comes from being in a relationship with a man.

Why tell you this? The world I have described disappeared in English culture during the 1980s. In 1947 a Gallup survey among women found in answer to the question: 'would you rather be male or female?' that only 56 per cent of women chose female. Today in response to the same question, a resounding 86 per cent prefer to be female.[1] Things have changed. Girls today grow up with fantastic role models. The world of fantasy fiction has provided us with Hermione Granger, Katniss Everdeen and Tris Prior. The *Star Wars* franchise has given us Ray, a heroine who wields the lightsaber herself. Schools encourage girls to take education very seriously, and girls outperform boys at GCSE and A-Level. More young

1   'Most women in 2016 happy to be female, BBC poll suggests' http://www.bbc.co.uk/news/uk-37600771 accessed July 2017

women go to university than men, and they outnumber men studying medicine and law. They are even beginning to break into engineering.

I grew up believing that, as a woman, I was second class while young women today grow up being told they have great potential. However, despite this, many find life is a lot more unsatisfying than they hoped and the world a more threatening and abusive place than they had been told. Others face broken relationships and struggle from the start. Modern life is a struggle. We have been told that we can be anything, but fear that we aren't enough in anything at all. We are aware of our inadequacies, our failings, and our inability to be what we dream of being. We feel the pressure to conform, to achieve, to be beautiful, to be capable, to be self-sufficient, to multitask, to have it all and do it all. We have been busy trying to gain respect and equality but are left gasping for something and not even sure what it is we need. Despite all our accomplishments, deep down, we know we need more. All of us in our darkest moments wonder what it means to be truly loved, really valued, and completely satisfied.

Scriptwriter Phoebe Waller-Bridge expressed a lot of people's fears through one of her characters:

I want someone to tell me what to wear in the morning......every morning, what to eat...what to like, what to hate, what to rage about, what to listen to, what band to like, what to buy tickets for, what to joke about, what not to joke about. I want someone to tell me what to believe in. Who to vote for, who to love, and how to tell them. I just think I want someone to tell me how to

*live my life because so far I think I have been getting it wrong...
I'm still scared. Why am I still scared?*[2]

Waller-Bridge's character in her exhausted pain longed for someone to take over. C.S. Lewis diagnosed this pain as our need to have a relationship with our creator:

If I find in myself a desire which no experience in this world can satisfy, the most probable explanation is that I was made for another world.[3]

But can it possibly be true that it is by knowing God that we can discover what it is to be truly loved? Can it be that by understanding the value God places on us we find out our true worth? Modern women are left with a dilemma, if the church has failed to love, value and respect women in the past, how can it be possible that Christianity has any answers to our deepest fears? We need to stop looking at the flawed institution of the church and start by looking at its great founder, the man Jesus Christ. How did Jesus view women, and what did He offer them?

Jesus' Encounters with Women

Women's status in the ancient world was low. The Athenian woman was unable to go into the public sphere without being accompanied by a trustworthy male escort; she was not permitted to eat with her husband's male guests, she was not given a voice, not allowed to engage in public discourse,

2   *Fleabag* season 2 broadcast on BBC in 2019
3   C.S. Lewis, *Mere Christianity* (1952), (Fount Paperbacks, 1984), p. 118

and not given access to education. It is no wonder that Euripides gave these famous words to Medea in his play of the same name: 'Surely, of all creatures that have life and wit, we women are of all unhappiest.'[4] Roman women had a little more freedom than their Greek counterparts, but their status was extremely low. Baby girls were considered disposable, and there were high rates of female infanticide. The early church was committed to the value of every life, and their rescue of these baby girls is well documented.[5]

At the time of Jesus' life and ministry Hebrew culture had many similarities in its attitude towards women, 'they were defined as socially, intellectually and spiritually inferior'. Jesus came into a culture that was at best respectful of the women in their family contexts but at worst, deeply misogynistic. Women had little influence, and they were not spoken to in public settings. The rabbinic oral law included this: 'Let the words of the Law be burned rather than taught to women...If a man teaches his daughter the Law, it is as though he taught her lechery.'[6]

Jesus came as God Himself, the one who gave life to the world, the one who had spoken everything into existence. He came to expose the darkness of that world and reveal the light. He confronted wrong understandings and challenged the leading theologians of His day. He accused them of 'setting aside the commands of God and holding on to human

4   *Medea,* 231-32, in Alvin J. Schmidt, *How Christianity changed the world* (Zondervan, 2014), pp. 98-99

5   ibid. p. 53

6   ibid. pp.103-104

traditions'.[7] When He burst on the scene, it caused such upset that it wasn't long before the Jewish leaders were plotting to kill Him.[8] His teaching and behaviour was radical, not least in how He related to women. He didn't exclude women from theological discussions, in fact, He engaged with women on some of the most important issues of the day. When He met a Samaritan woman in a place called Sychar, He broke every social taboo in the book.[9] Talking to her was radical in and of itself, but she was a despised foreigner with a very dubious moral background. His disciples were shocked to find Him speaking with a woman. If they had known the contents of the conversation, they would have been speechless. Jesus discussed the complex theological divisions between the Jews and the Samaritans and revealed to this woman the nature of true worship. But He did not just engage in an intellectually demanding conversation; His passionate concern was to offer this woman what He called 'the water of life'. He did not want her to be spiritually thirsty but to have a relationship with God the Father which would completely satisfy, unlike any other relationship she had experienced. He wanted to give her 'living water' which would lead to eternal life. It was an incredible conversation which culminated in Jesus telling her that He was the promised King that both the Jews and the Samaritans were waiting for. He revealed Himself as the promised Messiah to one of the most socially and politically insignificant people of His time. This woman mattered, she

---

7   Mark 7:9

8   Mark 3:6

9   John 4:4-30

mattered a lot. Jesus showed time again that women were important to Him. He taught them, they were numbered among His followers, and amazingly, when He rose from the dead He appeared first to a woman.

You might wonder how come women were generally so disregarded in Jesus' day. How had it got to this point? Some think the justification for women being viewed as less valuable comes straight from the pages of the Jewish Scriptures – the book we commonly refer to as the Old Testament. However, Jesus Himself upheld these Scriptures. He was adamant that He had come not to overturn them but to fulfil them.[10] If the Old Testament is a sexist text that leads to patriarchy and misogyny, it is strange that Jesus spoke so highly of it. It could be that Jesus was inconsistent, but that would be a problem too. If we are to trust Jesus, who offered the unnamed Samaritan woman life, we need to know that He is not inconsistent. We need to look at the book Jesus upheld. We need to find out if the Old Testament is to blame for a deep-seated hatred towards women. It stands accused of being a book that has been used to establish male power and confine women.

It is difficult to conclude that the Jesus we meet in the gospels supported teaching that was derogatory towards women, so could it be that the misogyny that we fear is in its pages is not there? Could it be that it is the traditions of men, not the Word of God, that is the heart of the problem? The rest of this book will explore what God's attitude to women is from the Old Testament, a book which many of us find alien

---

10   Matthew 5:17

and unsettling. Come with me on a journey back to where everything started.

For Further Thought and Conversation

- In the last 100 years activists have achieved a lot. What issues do you think women still need to deal with today?
- What do you think is essential in life in order for us to be fulfilled?

Read John 4:1-42

- What is Jesus offering the woman at the well?
- How does she respond to Him?
- What do you make of what Jesus offers?

2 MADE IN GOD'S IMAGE: GENESIS 1

During the 'Women of the World Festival', Gemma Cairney interviewed girls between the ages of 11–15 years about their experience of girlhood and found they placed huge importance on their appearance.[1] One girl described how it took her an hour to put her make-up on for school before she had the confidence to leave the house. Another talked about putting her selfies through software to remove her flaws to get more 'likes' on Instagram. When the group was asked if they considered themselves beautiful, they laughed at the idea and said: 'No'. And it is not just women who struggle with their image; young men also battle with the pressure to conform to stereotypes of the perfect physique. Adolescence insecurity, combined with our image-obsessed culture is a toxic combination. The playwright Charlotte Josephine argued that publishing images online increases vulnerability: 'I need

1   WOW – Women of the World Festival 2015 | WOW NOW with
     Gemma Cairney, youtube.com accessed June 2017

to look attractive, or I'm worthless, I am not enough.'[2] But getting our sense of worth and dignity from our appearance is illusive.

A Sense of Worth

Getting value from appearance is not a new problem. Simone de Beauvoir wrote about women's need to conform to the 'male gaze'.[3] Mary Wollstonecraft longed for women to be freed from what she called 'a gilt cage' by being allowed to expand their minds through education. She observed that many of her female contemporaries were doomed to becoming silly, frivolous and superficial because: 'they have been taught from their infancy that beauty is woman's sceptre.'[4] Mary Wollstonecraft knew that women had far greater capacities than her society allowed them to develop. To reduce women's significance to appearance is to miss their intrinsic value. No one would dispute this today. We know worth is not bestowed by online approval ratings, or the male/female gaze, nor even through educational attainment.

The Bible teaches that our value is intrinsic because God made us as His image-bearers. Both male and female display the image of God in beautiful symmetry and equality. However, this essential truth has, at various times in history,

2   Radio 4 BBC, *Women's hour,* 13 June 2017

3   Simone de Beauvoir, *The Second Sex* (1949) (Vintage, 1997)

4   Mary Wollstonecraft is widely regarded as the founding feminist philosopher. She wrote *A Vindication of the Rights of Men* (1790) and *A Vindication of the Rights of Woman,* (1792) (Cambridge University Press, 1995), p. 75

been turned on its head. Augustine (354-430) interpreted the creation of men and women like this:

> *not the woman but the man is the image of God ... human nature itself, which is complete [only] in both sexes, was made in the image of God; and it does separate the woman from the image of God which it signifies...The woman together with her own husband is the image of God, so that the whole substance may be one image; but when she is referred to separately in her quality of helpmate, which regards the woman herself alone, then she is not the image of God; but as regards the man alone, he is the image of God as fully and completely as when the woman too is joined with him.*[5]

This teaching influenced the church. The following was written in 1140:

> *The image of God is in man, and it is one. Women were drawn from man, who has God's jurisdiction as it were God's vicar because he has the image of the one God. Therefore woman is not made in God's image. Woman's authority is nil; let her in all things be subject to the rule of man.*[6]

Augustine was a brilliant theologian who produced outstanding teaching, but he was also a man of his time (no one gets it right all the time). Surely a woman hearing this couldn't help thinking that God considers her less than a man and not of equal worth. This teaching must have created insecurity far worse than being stuck in a social media rabbit

5   From Augustine, On the Holy Trinity, cited in: Julia O'Faolain, and Lauro Martines, *Not in God's Image* (London:Virago,1979), p. 142

6   From *Corpus Iuris Canonici*, cited in ibid. p. 143

hole. It fundamentally undermines women. Women coming across it now are at first incredulous and then angry at the implications of it. We know that this kind of teaching has impacted women's lives in the past and silenced their voices.

It is both sad and astonishing that the Bible has been interpreted this way because equality of the sexes is the starting point of the Bible story and the foundational truth about humanity:

Then God said, 'Let us make mankind in our image, in our likeness, so that they may rule over the fish in the sea and the birds in the sky, over the livestock and all the wild animals, and over all the creatures that move along the ground.'

So God created mankind in his own image,
  in the image of God he created them;
  male and female he created them.[7]

It is hard to express the importance of this. We are all valuable whatever our social status, whatever our intellect, whatever our talents, whatever our wealth, whatever our race, and whatever our body shape. These few lines establish the staggering complexity and dignity of humankind. Everything God made was good, but humanity was made in God's image and set apart from the rest of creation. People have extraordinary worth and privilege. This privilege extends to both male and female, together they are one humanity. There is a biological difference, male and female, but it is undefined. The idea highlighted here is 'image'. So what does being made

---

7   Genesis 1:26-27

in God's image mean? Milton imagined this scene in his epic poem 'Paradise Lost':

Two of far nobler shape erect and tall,
Godlike erect, with native honour clad,
In naked majesty seemed lords of all,
And worthy seemed, for in their looks divine
The image of their glorious maker[8]

Milton's poem described it as: 'looks divine' but the word 'image' in this context is not referring to how we look. Being made in the image of God is about relationships. Humanity was created to represent God and reflect the distinct qualities of God. It is as though people are ambassadors on earth for God. Rabbi Lord Jonathan Sacks put it like this:

In the ancient world, it was the rulers, emperors, and pharaohs who were held to be in the image of God. So what Genesis was saying was that we are all royalty. [9]

Nancy R. Pearcey concludes: 'The early readers of Genesis knew the text was making the astonishing claim that all humans, not just rulers, are representatives of God on earth.'[10]

It is as though we are all royalty, bestowed with extraordinary significance. We are God's representatives called to rule over the earth, and in doing so, we reflect God's image, the ultimate ruler. God reigns supremely over everything, but He has given

---

8   John Milton, *Paradise Lost, book iv* (Oxford World's Classics, 2004) p. 93

9   Cited in Nancy R. Pearcey *Love Thy Body* (Baker Books, 2018) p. 36

10   Ibid.

humanity an extraordinary calling under His authority. And take note, women are included in this. And in case we missed it, the delegation of authority and responsibility is repeated:

God blessed them and said to them, 'Be fruitful and increase in number; fill the earth and subdue it. Rule over the fish in the sea and the birds in the sky and over every living creature that moves on the ground.'[11]

There is nothing here to suggest that man is established as the ruler of creation without woman. There is no justification for saying: 'woman's authority is nil'. God spoke to both male and female; He blessed them and instructed them. He established equality between the sexes. Men and women are equally created by God, equal in dignity, and equal in worth. They are similarly tasked with procreation and equally needed: 'neither the man nor the woman can fill the earth and subdue it without the other'. There is a beautiful interdependence and mutuality here.

From the beginning, the Bible clearly shows that both men and women are valuable. Both reflect God's image, and both are extraordinarily beautiful. When God rested from His work of creation after making humanity, it was no longer described as only 'good', but 'very good'. This is how God views His world. He established men and women as joint rulers of creation. He didn't discriminate and rejoiced in what He had made.

We have immense worth, but we know that this world is no longer the place of perfection that God rejoiced in at the

---

11   Genesis 1:28

dawn of creation. Ignoring and neglecting this foundational truth leaves us rootless and without security.

Many of us live without an awareness of our inherent worth because we have forgotten that we have been made by God. Our creation by God is the starting point that gives our lives meaning and purpose. Our significance is measured by the intention of our creator. He created us to have a relationship with Him and nothing less than that. Without God, we will ache for affirmation. Our solutions are feeble. We are not very good at affirming each other, and we are spectacular at criticising each other, holding up impossible ideals that we ourselves fail to achieve. The confidence that we struggle to achieve dissolves at the click of a mouse, and we are left craving acceptance and experiencing rejection. Consider this: God made us, and therefore, we have worth, value, dignity, and purpose. You are made in the image of God. What does that mean to you? Does it give you a glimmer of hope? A tiny whisper? A glimpse into meaning and value that stands beyond time and stretches into eternity? I hope you can begin to see how it might.

FOR FURTHER THOUGHT AND CONVERSATION

- Why do you think men and women have not been considered equal in the past?
- Where does your sense of equality come from?

READ GENESIS 1

- What strikes you about how God creates?

- Why do you think God speaks to humanity and not to any other created thing?
- What difference do you think it makes knowing God is our creator?

3 MADE FOR RELATIONSHIP: GENESIS 2

There is a story that does the rounds on the internet, and whether or not it is true, I don't know. It tells of an English professor who wrote the following statement without punctuation: 'a woman without her man is nothing'. The class were asked to rewrite it with the correct punctuation. The boys punctuated it in the following way: *A woman, without her man, is nothing*. While the girls wrote: *A woman: without her, man is nothing*. All the students punctuated the sentence correctly but according to their own unconscious bias. To suggest that unless a woman is in a relationship with a man she is worthless, is problematic, to say the least. It harks back to the time when a woman's worth was measured by her marriageability. For the girls to turn that idea on its head and relegate men to second class is funny but also sad. The truth is that in the healthiest societies, there is mutual respect between both sexes. When we value both sexes and seek to enable both to flourish, everyone benefits.

Nobel prize winner Malala Yousafzai, in her rallying cry for education for all girls observed: 'we cannot succeed when half of us are held back'.[1] When the world ignores and devalues half its population serious harm is caused. We cannot isolate ourselves from the opposite sex and expect to thrive. The Bible is clear about this: we were created to be in relationship male and female with one another, designed to be fruitful, to establish communities of people in relationship with our creator. There is no place for one sex claiming independence from the other. This is the reason that the beginning of Genesis contains not one, but two accounts of creation. These accounts are different but not contradictory. The first is written with poetic flourish highlighting the power of God's voice; 'And God said' is repeated over and over again. God is the magnificent creator whose very breath brings life from nothing and creates a spectacular universe which teems with life, all of which is good. The climax of creation is humanity, and when God had finished He declared 'it is very good'. The second narrative narrows its focus to look in detail at the creation of man and woman. To our modern ears, this story seems strange and hard to take seriously, but the ideas here are fundamental. First, let's see what we can establish by reading it as it appears in Genesis:

The Lord God took the man and put him in the Garden of Eden to work it and take care of it. And the Lord God commanded the man, 'You are free to eat from any tree in the garden; but

1   https://www.theguardian.com/world/2013/jul/12/malala-yousafzai-calls-free-education Last accessed May 2021.

you must not eat from the tree of the knowledge of good and evil, for when you eat from it you will certainly die.'

The Lord God said, 'It is not good for the man to be alone. I will make a helper suitable for him.'

Now the Lord God had formed out of the ground all the wild animals and all the birds in the sky. He brought them to the man to see what he would name them; and whatever the man called each living creature, that was its name. So the man gave names to all the livestock, the birds in the sky and all the wild animals.

But for Adam no suitable helper was found. So the Lord God caused the man to fall into a deep sleep; and while he was sleeping, he took one of the man's ribs and then closed up the place with flesh. Then the Lord God made a woman from the rib he had taken out of the man, and he brought her to the man.

The man said,

'This is now bone of my bones
  and flesh of my flesh;
she shall be called "woman",
  for she was taken out of man.'

That is why a man leaves his father and mother and is united to his wife, and they become one flesh.

Adam and his wife were both naked, and they felt no shame.[2]

---

2   Genesis 2:15-25

In this second creation story something is not right. Up until this point, everything has been described as good, but now there is a problem: it is not good for man to be alone. Despite the variety and company of thousands of creatures, the experience of man is that he is alone. Animals cannot establish community. You may love animals and maybe find some preferable to some people you know. As I write, my labrador is lying at my feet, and I confess I am very attached to her. I love her company on walks and her enthusiastic greeting when I come home. I admit her habit of waking at 6.30 am every day is annoying, and she is known as the golden alarm clock, but I wouldn't want to be without her. However, she is not a substitute for my family or friends. She will curl up beside me when I watch TV but cannot offer any commentary, insight or humour which makes watching TV so much more fun. She has no understanding of what I am doing at my desk right now and cannot help me think more clearly or offer any helpful criticism. Dogs are great but even man's best friend has its limitations. This is clear from Genesis 2; animals were not enough. No other companion was suitable until there was one who was 'bone of my bones and flesh of my flesh'. No other companion would provide the relationship and intimacy that woman would bring.

Women As Less

However, many have read this passage as saying something quite negative about women. Naomi Wolf saw Genesis 2 as reinforcing the perception that women are 'second-rate' and 'second-class': 'Though God made Adam from clay, in his image, Eve is an expendable rib. God breathed life directly into Adam's nostrils, inspiring his body with divinity; but Eve's body is twice removed from the Maker's hand , imperfect matter born of matter.'[3]

Wolf's reading completely ignores the context of this passage. It is not pointing to the imperfection of woman; rather, it reveals the incompleteness of man, he was the one lacking – it is not good for man to be alone. The problem was not a problem with women but the fact that they were absent.

Why would a feminist be so suspicious of this story? Sadly, in the past some church leaders have used this passage negatively. It is not just modern readers who have read their framework into the story. Augustine wrote this:

> *If it were not the case that the woman was created to be man's helper specifically for the production of children, then why would she have been created as a 'helper'? Was it so that she might work the land with him? No . . . a male would have made a better assistant. One can also posit that the reason for her creation as a helper had to do with the companionship she could provide for the man . . . . Yet for company and conversation, how much more agreeable it is for two male friends to dwell together than for a man and a woman! . . . I cannot think of any reason for woman's being made as man's helper if we dismiss the reason of procreation.[4]*

---

3   Naomi Wolf, *The Beauty Myth* (Vintage: London, 1990) p. 93

4   Augustine, Literal Commentary on Genesis 9.5, quoted in Clark, Elizabeth A. Clark, *Women In the Early Church*, vol 13, *Message of the Fathers of the Church* (Wilmington, Del.: Michael Glazier, 1983), pp. 28-29.

And the reformer Martin Luther said:

> *Men have broad shoulders and narrow hips, and accordingly they possess intelligence. Women have narrow shoulders and broad hips. Women ought to stay at home; the way they were created indicates this, for they have broad hips and a wide fundament to sit upon, keep house and bear and raise children.*[5]

Is this what it means to be suitable? Is a woman made so that man can procreate? I can't help thinking that Luther was inconsistent. Luther depended on his extraordinary and intelligent wife, Katharina Von Bora who, in her time, managed to run a farm, a brewery, a hotel, a large estate and a hospital.[6]

Some of these views about women developed from understanding the phrase 'suitable helper' as meaning women were made to have babies and serve in the domestic sphere. But is this right? Was Eve created to cater for all of Adam's needs, have his children, make his meals, and do all his washing and cleaning? Was woman made to be Adam's chief cook and bottle washer? Milton, in his re-telling of this story, implies this, casting Eve as the beautiful domestic goddess chiefly concerned with how to please Adam by preparing delicious food. Milton's Eve adores cooking:

> *She turns, on hospitable thoughts intent*
> *What choice to choose for delicacy best,*
> *What order so contrived as not to mix*

5   Martin Luther *Table Talk* no.55 , cited in Julia O'Faolain,and Lauro Martines, *Not in God's image*, (Virago:London,1979), p. 209

6   Clare Heath-Whyte, *First Wives Club* (10publishing, 2014), p. 43

Tastes, not well joined, inelegant, but bring
Taste after taste upheld with kindliest change.[7]

Milton gave his stereotyped Eve qualities that conformed to his ideal of womanhood. He read Genesis through his cultural grid just as many have done before him and after him. Does the account in Genesis justify this re-imagining? It is an important question. Many consider that Genesis 2 is the point at which the Bible enslaves women; Stephen Pinker concludes that the Judea-Christian tradition establishes the following culture:

Women are derivative of men and destined to be ruled by them.[8]

Pinker observes that some traditional teaching has wrongly undermined women both in their personhood and position in society. It is true that religion has been used to restrict women to the domestic sphere pushing an expectation that their primary purpose was to marry and have babies. However, I am convinced that the Bible should not be blamed for this. In fact, it is a misrepresentation of Genesis 2. The story is not about Adam's need to have babies in order to be fruitful. It is addressing the question of being alone on a different level. The problem in chapter 2 was not the lack of a sexual partner; it was a profound aloneness. The issue at stake was man's need for a relationship with another corresponding to him,

---

7   John Milton, *Paradise Lost, book V. l:332-336*, (Oxford World's Classics, 2004) p. 124.

8   Stephen Pinker, *The Blank State* (Penguin Books, 2002) p. 1

someone who could be alongside him as they cared for the garden: 'The Lord God said, "It is not good for the man to be alone. I will make a helper suitable for him."'

A Suitable Helper

So how does this woman help the man if it's not about having babies and domesticity? It is easy to read the word 'helper' negatively, imagining that this means women are to be servants of men but the Hebrew translates into something much stronger. The word 'helper' is *'ezer'* and it is used to describe God's relationship with His people.[9] There is strength in this word: women are a strong helper or warrior helper.[10] This word gives us confidence that it is not describing someone who is an inferior sidekick or subservient to a superior being. The two Genesis creation accounts together show us that woman was created to work alongside man as his 'strong helper', and that together they share the task of procreation, ruling and subduing the creation.

SAMENESS

What stands out from this story is that men and women need one another. The joy Adam experienced when he met Eve is a beautiful thing, her response is not recorded, but their oneness – their unity – is. Nothing separates them, they are naked, vulnerable with each other, and there is no shame, no guilt. There is nothing here about how men and women are to function. This does not teach that women should remain

9   See Exodus 18:4, Deuteronomy 33:29, Psalm 33:20, Psalm 118:7

10   Ps 115:9-11

in the home, and men should be the wage earners. There is nothing here about any difference in the intellectual capacity between men and women. Men are not created intellectually superior to women. There is nothing here to describe the different characteristics of men and women, but a lot here that emphasises their similarity. The Bible establishes the shared humanity of men and women. Eve is the same as Adam and is celebrated in the world's first poem:

This is now bone of my bones
  and flesh of my flesh;
she shall be called 'woman',
  for she was taken out of man.

Adam rejoices in the sameness and the kinship he has with his wife. It is at this point in the narrative that the writer adds a comment: *'That is why a man leaves his father and mother and is united to his wife, and they become one flesh'.*

The marriage union is a kind of reunion. It acknowledges the bond between the man and the woman, the sameness, and the kinship. Their union is much more than a biological joining of two bodies. Nancy R. Pearcey describes it like this:

The reference to physical unity was intended to express a joyous unity on all other levels as well – including mind, emotion, and spirit. Scripture offers a stunningly high view of physical union as a union of whole persons across all dimensions.[11]

God's design for sex is about more than satisfying physical desire; it is about a deep communion between persons, a

---

11   Pearcey, *Love Thy Body*, p. 138

profound intimacy. It is a relationship that displays not only the closeness and commitment to the other, but it mirrors the relationship of God with His people. We will discover more about this in a later chapter.

MORE THAN MARRIAGE

We were not made to be alone. This first relationship became the foundation for all other relationships. Marriage is good but the foundational truth that Genesis teaches us goes beyond that. Our desire for love and intimacy, for companionship and trust, is hardwired within us. None of us can function alone: even the most isolated individual in our society who never speaks to another person depends on others every time they flick on a light switch. We need each other. John Donne famously wrote in his meditation: 'no man is an island, entire of itself; every man is a piece of the continent, a part of the main'.[12] We need each other to function practically and emotionally; loneliness and social isolation are harmful to our health. The pain many of us have experienced as a consequence of social lockdowns due to Covid is huge, we are reminded again and again that being alone is not good.

ALONE AGAIN

The creation stories end with this extraordinary scene:

Adam and his wife were both naked, and they felt no shame.

---

12 John Donne, (1624) *Devotions upon Emergent Occasions* (Oxford University Press, 1987)

It is hard for us to imagine the experience that Adam and Eve had in paradise because we live with the knowledge of shame. The perfection of Genesis 2 does not describe the world we know. We live with the experience of longing for closeness but struggling to be open with others. People let us down, and in turn, we hurt those we love and withdraw from them. We hide in our lies, not open to others, and not open before God. We feel shame. We have a deep longing. We want to be loved. We want to be known. We want to be vulnerable and feel no shame. This is a proper longing, the cry of the human heart. We were made for relationship with God and each other.

Some of us have been so hurt that we have given up trusting anyone; others of us readily believe everyone but are let down over and over again. God knows the brokenness with which we live. The Bible story is about God restoring us to a relationship with Himself and with one another. He loves us more deeply than we can ever know. His offer to us is so rich it is hard for us to comprehend. John, one of Jesus' disciples, described it like this:

> *See what great love the Father has lavished on us, that we should be called children of God!*[13]

The love that God lavishes on us will satisfy our most deep-seated need. He brings us back into a relationship with Himself but also with one another. The promise of God brings us not just into the Father's presence but into a new family of other believers. God cares about relationships. He does not want us to be alone.

---

13   1 John 3:1

For Further Thought and Conversation

- Do you think loneliness is a problem in our culture?
- What stops us having close friendships?
- Why is it difficult to have healthy friendships between men and women?
- What stereotypes do we have of men and women?

Read Genesis 2:4-25

- Why does God give the man a command not to eat from the tree of knowledge of good and evil?
- According to the story, what is the significance of the woman being made from man's rib?
- From this chapter, what does God want for men and women?

4 MESSING UP THE DESIGN: GENESIS 3

What is the worst thing that you have ever been accused of? One of the worst charges levelled against women, in general, is that made by the church father, Tertullian:

> *You are the devil's gateway: you are the unsealer of that (forbidden) tree: you are the first deserter of the divine law: you are she who persuaded him whom the devil was not valiant enough to attack. You destroyed so easily God's image, man. On account of your desert – that is, death – even the Son of God had to die. And you think about adorning yourself over and above your 'tunics of skins'.[1]*

Simone de Beauvoir believed that women have always been hated by men and that: 'all Christian literature strives to enhance the disgust that man can feel for a woman'.[2] She saw Tertullian's teaching in particular as proving her point. You

---

1   Tertullian, 'On the dress of Women,' quoted in Sarah Sumner, *Men and Women in the Church* (IVP, 2003), p. 41

2   De Beauvoir, *The Second Sex*, p. 199

can hear the disgust in his words: 'you are the devil's gateway, responsible for the downfall of man, the ones who destroyed the perfection of Eden, the reason that the Son of God had to die'. This is a huge burden to bear – I cannot think of a more awful accusation.

Personally, I have never heard any church leader espouse this kind of sentiment today, but they have in the past. Terrifying opinions about women have been derived from Scripture. Elizabeth Cady Stanton, the American suffragist, saw the Bible as responsible for the diminished position of women in her society. She produced *The Woman's Bible* to counter it. She caused a split in the suffragist movement because many other women did not share her view that the Bible was the reason for the misogyny she described. These women were so shocked by her ideas that they issued a formal denunciation of her book and distanced themselves from her. There were many within the early suffragist movement who did not hold the Bible as responsible for the lack of rights that they experienced.

The Bible has been used and abused to promote any number of unjust causes, but that does not justify rejecting it and refusing to take it seriously. In fact, the converse is true. We should treat the Bible with great care and seriousness because it is such an influential book. We need to try and understand what it says, being careful not to push ideas further than the Bible itself does. How we read the Bible story matters.

In our last chapter, we read about the perfection in Eden; but we know that's not what the world is like now. Paradise is lost. So how did that happen? And who is to blame? Is it, in fact, Eve? Does the Bible blame her for bringing sin and death into the world? Indeed in the Bible, Eve is held responsible for her actions. Paul writes: *'and Adam was not the one deceived; it was the woman who was deceived and became a sinner'.*[3] However, this does not excuse Adam; elsewhere, Paul speaks of Adam's responsibility in leading humanity into sin, death, and judgement.

> *Therefore, just as sin entered the world through one man, and death through sin, and in this way death came to all people, because all sinned.*[4]

> *Through the disobedience of the one man the many were made sinners.* [5]

Paul was not saying that women are more susceptible than men; rather, he was describing events in the Genesis narrative. Adam and Eve share responsibility, but their sin is defined differently: Eve was deceived, and Adam was disobedient. Both are guilty.

How did Paul come to this conclusion? Let's read the story of how it all went wrong.

The Fall

> *Now the snake was more crafty than any of the wild animals the Lord God had made. He said to the woman, 'Did God really say, "You must not eat from any tree in the garden"?'*

---

3   1 Timothy 2:14

4   Romans 5:12

5   Romans 5:19

The woman said to the snake, 'We may eat fruit from the trees in the garden, but God did say, "You must not eat fruit from the tree that is in the middle of the garden, and you must not touch it, or you will die."'

'You will not certainly die,' the snake said to the woman. 'For God knows that when you eat from it your eyes will be opened, and you will be like God, knowing good and evil.'

When the woman saw that the fruit of the tree was good for food and pleasing to the eye, and also desirable for gaining wisdom, she took some and ate it. She also gave some to her husband, who was with her, and he ate it. Then the eyes of both of them were opened, and they realised that they were naked; so they sewed fig leaves together and made coverings for themselves.

Then the man and his wife heard the sound of the Lord God as he was walking in the garden in the cool of the day, and they hid from the Lord God among the trees of the garden. But the Lord God called to the man, 'Where are you?'

He answered, 'I heard you in the garden, and I was afraid because I was naked; so I hid.'

And he said, 'Who told you that you were naked? Have you eaten from the tree from which I commanded you not to eat?'

The man said, 'The woman you put here with me – she gave me some fruit from the tree, and I ate it.'

Then the Lord God said to the woman, 'What is this you have done?'

The woman said, 'The snake deceived me, and I ate.' [6]

---

6   Genesis 3:1-13

Eve talked with one of the creatures in the garden. Bear with me here, I know this sounds mythological and fanciful, but the Bible treats this passage with the utmost seriousness. It is not a fairy story. This event is the backdrop to everything that follows in the Bible story. We may struggle with the concept of a talking snake, and find it hard to believe. Francis Schaeffer explained it like this:

> *The Bible is a book for fallen people. Wherever it touches upon anything, it does so with true truth, but not with exhaustive truth. – When the Bible talks about the supernatural world and tells us of heaven and things beyond this earth, they stand as corollaries to the theme of the book – the propositional communication in verbalised form from God to fallen people. The corollaries given are those we need to know to get the major thrust, the central purpose of the Bible. But it does not answer every question that we might ask about any of these matters.*[7]

This story is told in a way that from generation to generation, we can understand it. The purpose of Genesis 3 is to examine what went wrong in a form that everyone can understand. The writer of the book of Revelation helps us a little more by explicitly describing the snake as Satan:

> *The great dragon was hurled down – that ancient snake called the devil, or Satan, who leads the whole world astray. He was hurled to the earth, and his angels with him.*[8]

---

7   Francis A. Schaeffer, *Genesis in Time and Space* (Hodder and Stoughton, 1972), p. 76

8   Revelation 12:9

Eve was engaged in conversation with Satan. She was encouraged to doubt what she had been told by Adam. Adam had clearly been told:

> *You are free to eat from any tree in the garden; but you must not eat from the tree of the knowledge of good and evil, for when you eat from it you will certainly die.* [9]

Satan twisted this to make God's restriction seem harsh. Eve's initial response was quite good. She corrected Satan. She knew that she enjoyed enormous freedom to eat from anything except the one tree. However, she went on to exaggerate the command God had given by adding that she must not even touch the tree, although there is nothing in the narrative that suggests that this is true. God's command to Adam was all about eating. Having succeeded in causing Eve to doubt God's goodness, Satan then struck. He twisted what God had said, declaring that Eve would not die if she ate the fruit. He was effectively accusing God of being a power-crazy liar. It is the ultimate deception: to believe God is not good. Sadly, Eve was taken in and in an ironic twist saw the fruit as good when, in reality, it was deadly. She was deceived, deluded into thinking it would give her knowledge, making her like God. So she took it and ate it.

Throughout history, this rejection of God's Word has replayed again and again. God has spoken, but we doubt it. God has our best interests at heart, but we become convinced that He is untrustworthy, egotistical, and restricts our freedom. In our desire for more, we fear He wants less for us.

9   Genesis 2:16-17

How easy it is to doubt God's goodness and reject Him. Eve doubted God's goodness, and that led to her disobedience and ultimate downfall. How like her we all are! Over and over, we are deceived. We too fail to check what God really said and see what God is really like. Eve may have been the first, but she was not the last. She needed to know God could be trusted, and she should have known. She had been living in paradise: God's beautiful garden in which there was no guilt or shame, no sin or death. She had experienced a perfect relationship with God. She and Adam had walked with Him in the cool of the day. Despite this, she chose to listen to Satan's lies. We don't live in Eden, but we can see God's power in creation but, like Eve, we suppress the truth and, like Eve, are held culpable. The Bible describes us like this:

> *The wrath of God is being revealed from heaven against all the godlessness and wickedness of people, who suppress the truth by their wickedness, since what may be known about God is plain to them, because God has made it plain to them. For since the creation of the world God's invisible qualities – his eternal power and divine nature – have been clearly seen, being understood from what has been made, so that people are without excuse.*[10]

Does this description fit? Do we frequently think that God is repressive and restrictive and not good for us? Do we doubt that God has our best interests at heart? Do we have an inborn tendency to ignore the evidence of God's character and push what we know about Him to one side? The Bible is

---

10   Romans 1: 18-20

uncompromising in how it presents Eve because she represents us all, man and woman alike. We need to ask ourselves if we are the same. Do we doubt God's Word? Do we trust that God is good? Eve had a lot of evidence to help her land the right way on these questions, but she failed. You may think that Eve had it easy as she saw God walking in the cool of the day, whereas we live centuries later. But we have evidence too. We have God revealing Himself through the pages of the Bible, a book that we can access more than at any time in human history: a book that sits unread in many rooms, a book that can be read online for free, a book that can be listened to through an app, a book that contains so much more than Eve ever saw. She did not get to see or hear the eye-witness stories about the man Jesus Christ, the Word made flesh, who died for us and was raised from the dead. The truth is we ignore the evidence just like Eve did.

Eve was responsible for being deceived, but what about Adam? Adam was guilty because not only had he been taught directly and explicitly the command of God, he was a witness and observer to the drama as it played out and yet he did nothing. He did not intervene or rebuke Satan, instead, he ate the fruit too.

> *When the woman saw that the fruit of the tree was good for food and pleasing to the eye, and also desirable for gaining wisdom, she took some and ate it. She also gave some to her husband, who was with her, and he ate it.*

Adam had the opportunity to turn things around, but instead, he was silently drawn in. He abdicated responsibility for holding fast to what he knew and had been commanded and colluded with Eve. He was condemned for this:

> *To Adam he said, 'Because you listened to your wife and ate fruit from the tree about which I commanded you, "You must not eat from it"'...*[11]

There were immediate consequences for them both:

> *Then the man and his wife heard the sound of the Lord God as he was walking in the garden in the cool of the day, and they hid from the Lord God among the trees of the garden. But the Lord God called to the man, 'Where are you?' He answered, 'I heard you in the garden, and I was afraid because I was naked; so I hid.'*

Everything changed; even the sound of God approaching became a source of fear. So they hid. Previously they had no experience of shame, but now they were aware of their nakedness. They were desperate to try and fix themselves with pathetic coverings. Both the man and the woman were exposed, neither was more guilty or more fallen than the other. Before the holy God, all they could do was a pathetic attempt to hide. It was tragic and terrible, but God did not reject them outright. He confronted them and then provided for them:

> *The Lord God made garments of skin for Adam and his wife and clothed them. And the Lord God said, 'The man has now become like one of us, knowing good and evil. He must not be*

---

11   Genesis 3:17

allowed to reach out his hand and take also from the tree of life and eat, and live for ever.' [12]

In their despair, God showed them mercy, even though their relationship with Him needed fixing. But this event had enormous consequences for them and all future generations.

Consequences

God confronted the man with a simple question: 'have you eaten from the tree from which I commanded you not to eat?' The man answered by blaming the woman for what he had done, and implying that ultimately God was the one responsible: 'it's not my fault – it was her; actually it's your fault for making her'. An excuse that echoes through time: 'I can't be held responsible for my actions, others led me into it. Anyway, God made the world like this, so it's His fault'. Adam was defensive and divided from those that he had previously enjoyed fellowship with.

The woman comes across as more ambiguous; she admitted that she was deceived, but I can't help thinking she too was excusing herself: 'it's not my fault, I was misled. I genuinely believed what I had been told by the snake. It's the snake that's the liar.' In this she was right, Jesus describes the devil as 'the father of lies',[13] however being led astray is not a defence before God. Despite their appeals, both Adam and Eve were guilty and experienced a new separation. There was now a gulf between each other and between them and God. They were

12   Genesis 3:21-22

13   John 8:44

in a hopeless situation, but it was the snake that God turned to first.

> *So the Lord God said to the snake, 'Because you have done this,*
>
> *'Cursed are you above all livestock*
> *and all wild animals!*
> *You will crawl on your belly*
> *and you will eat dust*
> *all the days of your life.*
> *And I will put enmity*
> *between you and the woman,*
> *and between your offspring and hers;*
> *he will crush your head,*
> *and you will strike his heel.'*[14]

This is not the story of how the snake lost its legs. It's the story of how Satan's head will be crushed. It predicts his eventual destruction. This is a promise that one day, someone would come who would defeat Satan. Satan would inflict an injury on this someone: 'you will strike his heel', but the one to come would have the final victory: 'he will crush your head'. Right at the outset of humanity's rebellion, God speaks of two consequences; the first is an ongoing battle with evil, but the second brings the hope of rescue and the defeat of Satan. In just a few words, a central focus of the Bible is seen: the rescue of people from Satan's grasp. Jesus is the one that was promised. He is the offspring. When He was crucified, He was injured by Satan, but not destroyed. He is the one

---

14   Genesis 3:14-15

who defeated Satan on the cross, and He is the one who will overthrow Satan utterly. We look forward to that day.

For Adam and Eve, that time was way off, and they would have to get used to living in a broken world experiencing conflict, chaos, and evil as day-to-day realities. This is a world we know only too well.

How do you feel about these beginning chapters of Genesis? Does the story of the fall of humanity seem like a foolish myth to you? The more I examine it, the more convinced I am by it. It describes the reality I experience. Evil exists. We cannot get away from that fact. We may live in insulated environments enjoying relative security, success, and prosperity, but we know it is temporary – death lies ahead. All of us know what it is to be hurt by others; we know what it is to be lied to. Many of us have been the victim of a crime, some minor, some horrendous. The most privileged of us make sure we lock and double lock everything, and we have numerous passwords and security procedures. When we peep out from our fragile insulated bubbles, we see a world that is hurting deeply. When we listen to the news, read blogs, follow websites, there is so much pain, and ongoing injustice, that it is hard to look. Art, music, films, and literature shout about our brokenness or seek to provide temporary respite. I once studied with an English professor who was an atheist, yet he loved 'Paradise Lost' and Genesis because he was convinced they described reality as we experience it. Genesis 3 points to the truth about our world, ourselves, and our distance from God. It defines us all. Do you recognise this?

Women are not more fallen than men. The Bible does not say that, but it does claim that we are all profoundly damaged, male and female. When you look into yourself, do you see perfection or brokenness? We are used to living as fallen people, and we find ways to cope with ourselves. Few of us are as bad as we could be, and most of us mask our pain. But when we dare to look what do we see? Do you know that isolation from others and God? Do you fear exposure? Do you ache for rescue? There is hope in the Bible story, but before we look at the relief God provides, we need to look deeper into the consequences and horror of the fall. That is the subject of the next chapter.

For Further Thought and Conversation
- In what way does God display His eternal power and divine nature to us today?
- Do you think that we often ignore the evidence of God's character and push what we know about Him to one side?
- What does it mean to you that the world is fallen?

Read Genesis 3
- Why do you think Adam and Eve listened to the snake?
- Why do you think they hid from God?
- What do you expect God to do about this?

5 THE FALLOUT

In December 2015 the UK brought into force a new offence of controlling or coercive behaviour in intimate relationships.[1] A conviction carries a maximum sentence of five years imprisonment, a fine or both. The domestic abuse charity Women's Aid welcomed the change as a landmark moment after years of campaigning. They said in a statement:

> Coercive control is at the heart of domestic abuse... Women's Aid and other organisations campaigned to have this recognised in law, and we are thrilled that this has now happened.[2]

However, Sandra Horley of Refuge, another women's charity, expressed a concern:

---

1   Home Office *Controlling or Coercive Behaviour in Intimate or Family relationships*   https://www.gov.uk/government/uploads/system/uploads/attachment_data/file/482528/Controlling_or_coercive_behaviour_-_statutory_guidance.pdf Last accessed May 2021.

2   http://www.independent.co.uk/news/uk/home-news/everything-you-need-to-know-about-the-new-psychological-abuse-law-a6789271.html Last accessed May 2021.

> *The police don't even arrest when there is evidence of serious physical violence, so how are police and juries ever going to understand complex concepts like coercive control?*[3]

What no one denied was that psychological abuse is a serious problem. Everyone also knew that although the law applied to all intimate and family relationships, the vast majority of victims were women. Women have suffered abuse at the hands of men throughout history, and it continues today. Domestic violence is an ugly reality. It is one of the seismic consequences of the fall.

After the fall everything was damaged, paradise was lost. Paul, in one of his letters, described it as creation being subjected to frustration and in bondage to decay.[4] All of the areas of responsibility that humanity had: the tasks of ruling, subduing, and filling the earth remained; but now they involved struggle and hardship.

Ruling the earth would be challenged by a powerful and aggressive enemy, the devil, who is described in various places as:

> *A murderer from the beginning, not holding to the truth, for there is no truth in him. When he lies, he speaks his native language, for he is a liar and the father of lies.*[5]

> *A roaring lion looking for someone to devour.*[6]

---

3   ibid.

4   Romans 8:20-21

5   John 8:44

6   1 Peter 5:8

Satan, who leads the whole world astray.[7]

Subduing the earth would involve painful toil and sweat. The ground itself was now resistant to man's labour, producing thorns and thistles instead of abundant crops. Satisfying and fruitful work would not come without struggle:

> *To Adam he said, 'Because you listened to your wife and ate fruit from the tree about which I commanded you, "You must not eat from it,"*
>
> *'Cursed is the ground because of you;*
>   *through painful toil you will eat food from it*
>   *all the days of your life.*
> *It will produce thorns and thistles for you,*
>   *and you will eat the plants of the field.*
> *By the sweat of your brow*
>   *you will eat your food*
> *until you return to the ground,*
>   *since from it you were taken;*
> *for dust you are*
>   *and to dust you will return.'*[8]

Likewise filling the earth became difficult. The woman had been given the unique role of bearing children, and although her experience of giving birth would bring joy, it would only be achieved through painful labour:

> *To the woman he said,*
> *'I will make your pains in childbearing very severe;*
>   *with painful labour you will give birth to children.*

---

7   Revelation 12:9

8   Genesis 3:17-19

Your desire will be for your husband,
  and he will rule over you."[9]

It is not that women were singled out for suffering; everything was damaged, subject to frustration, pain, and struggle. Adam and Eve's act of disobedience brought death and decay; it was the thing that God had warned Adam about.

The destruction of the relationship between man and woman is described in appalling terms:

Your desire will be for your husband,
  and he will rule over you.'

Woman it seems was destined to be under the thumb of man, and the battle of the sexes began. Misogyny, sexism, and oppression begin here. These thirteen simple words explain the subjugation of millions of women through the centuries. However, these words need to be carefully understood. Let's start with the word 'desire'.

When we think of desire, we think of feelings of longing, usually sexual longing but this is not what it means here. We can understand it better by looking at how the same Hebrew word for 'desire' is used in the next chapter with striking parallels:

Sin is crouching at your door; it desires to have you, but you must rule over it.[10]

---

9   Genesis 3:16

10   Genesis 4:7

Cain was in a battle with sin. The Lord told Cain that he must fight against it. Cain needed to use his force and strength to withstand the temptation he was about to face. When we look back at the phrase 'Your desire will be for your husband, and he will rule over you,' we can see that it is similar. These words describe a struggle for control, and mastery: a battle of the sexes. The glorious equality and unity which had existed between Adam and Eve beforehand lay in tatters; instead of a united alliance, there was now a competitive disharmony. Here are the seeds of all relationship breakdowns. In fact, in the very next chapter, we see Cain fail to fight sin – instead he commits the first murder, but sadly not the last. The ruin of relationships was not confined to gender-based violence.

Life became a nightmare for Adam and Eve and their future, hopeless. Death lay in wait for them as it does for us all, as the saying goes: 'the one thing we can be certain of is death and taxes'. The Bible describes death as our last enemy,[11] which holds us in fearful bondage.[12] Even if we manage to live a healthy life, free from sickness and decay, we still face death. If our work is a pleasure and brings personal and financial fulfilment, it will come to an end. If our family is close and friendships delightful, they will be torn apart by death. Death is a cruelty which comes too soon. As the world battles Coronavirus even the most prosperous societies have been reminded of their fragility and mortality. Our lives are like *'a mist that appears for a little while and then vanishes'.*[13]

---

11   1 Corinthians 15:26

12   Hebrews 2:15

13   James 4:14

The writer of Ecclesiastes advises: *'It is better to go to a house of mourning than to go to a house of feasting, for death is the destiny of everyone; the living should take this to heart'.[14]* We have tried to ignore death and hide it from view in regions of the world where life expectancy is increasing, but age and decay are inevitable. The next few chapters in the book of Genesis contain record-breaking lifespans of the generations that followed Adam and Eve, but the outcome was the same for them all: 'and then he died'. Death is inevitable; we cannot stop it. Apart from the one man who came to do just that:

> *For if, by the trespass of the one man, death reigned through that one man, how much more will those who receive God's abundant provision of grace and of the gift of righteousness reign in life through the one man, Jesus Christ![15]*

> *For since death came through a man, the resurrection of the dead comes also through a man.[16]*

This is extraordinary! The dead don't come back to life. And yet, Jesus did. Many saw Him. He died. I have been there when others have died, witness to the cold stiffness that comes following that last breath. The person has gone; there is no mistaking it. The feeling of loss and grief overwhelms and threatens to drown you. Can you imagine what it must have been like for the women who loved Jesus to watch Him be brutally murdered? Can you feel their agony as they watched His lifeless body being pulled down from the cross, and further

---

14   Ecclesiastes 7:2

15   Romans 5:17

16   1 Corinthians 15:21

mutilated as His side was pierced with a sword? Can you feel their grief as others wrapped His body and hastily buried Him in a stranger's grave? This was the loss of the most astounding person they had known. All their hopes had been pinned on Him, and for it to end like this. Death had destroyed the only one who had offered life. The fear and amazement and disbelief must have been overwhelming when they found themselves once again in His presence. Death normally wins, but this time, death was defeated. The first to meet Jesus after His resurrection was a woman, Mary. It shouldn't have been a surprise; Jesus had explained to Martha just a few weeks earlier that He was the one who would reverse the curse of death:

> I am the resurrection and the life. The one who believes in me will live, even though they die; and whoever lives by believing in me will never die.[17]

Is this something that you can believe? Many witnesses saw Jesus raised from the dead. It is a fact that changes everything. I wonder what you make of it? You may not be convinced, but I urge you to check it out. Why not read the story of Jesus' resurrection in full?[18] Jesus came to defeat death; life is God's ultimate goal for us. It is hard for us to grasp, but eternity is a reality, and Jesus' resurrection displays its certainty.

Back in Genesis 3, Adam and Eve had to face death and the ugliness of living in a world without God. They had to experience 'the knowledge of good and evil' in all of its brutality. It seemed as though everything good was lost.

---

17   John 11:25-26

18   John 20

However, even as they left the garden, there was a glimmer of hope. Eve was confirmed as the one who would become the mother of all the living. God's purpose for them was not completely lost, they were to continue to subdue, rule, and fill the earth together. The Lord God gave them clothes which He made for them. At the end of the chapter, although they were barred from the tree of life, it was not because God wanted to deny them life but to preserve them for life. God knew that both Adam and his newly named wife Eve required a lasting change before they would be ready to eat from the tree of life. They were not to eat from this tree in their fallen condition. The tree of life appears again in the very last book of the Bible, the book of Revelation:

> Then the angel showed me the river of the water of life, as clear as crystal, flowing from the throne of God and of the Lamb down the middle of the great street of the city. On each side of the river stood the tree of life, bearing twelve crops of fruit, yielding its fruit every month. And the leaves of the tree are for the healing of the nations. No longer will there be any curse. The throne of God and of the Lamb will be in the city, and his servants will serve him. They will see his face, and his name will be on their foreheads.[19]

This is our hope. A day when all of the consequences of the fall are undone. A day made possible because Jesus the serpent crusher will have finally destroyed Satan. The curse of Genesis will be reversed, all the damage gone. It's a beautiful vision at the end of the Bible. It is a vision full of poetic language to

---

19   Revelation 22:1-4

help us imagine the glory of it. C.S. Lewis re-imagined it in his final Narnia story, *The Last Battle*, like this:

> *It is as hard to explain how this sunlit land was different from the old Narnia as it would be to tell you how the fruits of that country taste. Perhaps you will get some idea of it if you think of it like this. You may have been in a room in which there was a window that looked out on a lovely bay of the sea or a green valley that wound away among the mountains. And in the wall of that room opposite to the window there may have been a looking glass. And as you turned away from the window you suddenly caught sight of that sea or that valley all over again, in the looking glass. And the sea in the mirror, or the valley in the mirror, were in one sense just the same as the real ones: yet at the same time they were somehow different – deeper, more wonderful, more like places in a story – in a story you have never heard but very much want to know.*
>
> *The difference between the old Narnia and the new one was like that. The new one was a deeper country: every rock and flower and blade of grass looked as if it meant more. I can't describe it any better than that: if you ever get there you will know what I mean.*[20]

God's new creation will be so much more than we can imagine. But we are not there yet. Currently, we live in a messy world, with ripples of evil constantly lashing at our shores. Everything is not as bad as it could be: we are made in the image of God, and we do experience God's restraining hand and the goodness of His provision for us. There are moments

---

20   C.S. Lewis, *The Last Battle* (1956), (HarperCollins, 2009), p. 209-210

of staggering beauty in this creation, the love of family, the companionship of good friends, the artistry and creativity of our best musicians, writers, designers, and inventors. Yet the world groans in frustration and relationships break. Women certainly have had many reasons to groan. Much of this horror is described in the pages of the Old Testament. It is to these things that we will turn next.

FOR FURTHER THOUGHT AND CONVERSATION

- What do you consider to be the most significant problems facing our world?
- Why do you think that women have faced abuse throughout history?
- How does our culture view death?

READ JOHN 19:16-20:29

- What did the women see?
- What did Peter, John, and Thomas see?
- How can we believe without seeing with our own eyes?
- Why do Christians say that Jesus' resurrection is the most critical event in history?

6 HOW THE STORY UNFOLDS

The vast majority of people are bible illiterates. They only hear the palatable verses from the pulpit and blindly accept that the bible emanates goodness and is the word of God. Any honest, thinking person reading through the bible cannot ignore the blatant misogyny and barbarity towards women.[1]
– Atheist Foundation of Australia

The Bible is not comfortable reading. It can be confusing: many of its famous characters, rather than being exemplary, lead complicated and messy lives. It can be upsetting: there are descriptions of barbarity towards women. But the Bible was not written to give us examples of heroic figures and role models. The Bible describes life, in all of its reality and for many, their experience was as Thomas Hobbes observed: 'solitary, poore, nasty, brutish, and short'.[2] The Bible, however,

---

1   http://atheistfoundation.org.au/article/women-in-the-bible/   Last accessed May 2021

2   Thomas Hobbes (1588-1679), British philosopher. *Leviathan*, part 1, ch. 13 (1651)

does much more than describe our experience. Its claim is much greater. Paul described it like this:

> *The Holy Scriptures, which are able to make you wise for salvation through faith in Christ Jesus. All Scripture is God-breathed and is useful for teaching, rebuking, correcting, and training in righteousness, so that the servant of God may be thoroughly equipped for every good work.*[3]

The Bible is concerned with two things: providing knowledge of Jesus so we can receive His rescue, and then equipping us to serve Jesus. Paul was referring to the Old Testament when he wrote this, yet the Old Testament was written before Jesus was born. To say that the Old Testament (which is full of those famously difficult stories) is actually about Jesus is surprising. However, it's not just Paul who said so. Jesus Himself made the same claim: 'You study the Scriptures diligently because you think that in them you have eternal life. These are the very Scriptures that testify about me'.[4] So even the stories which we struggle with concerning women in the Old Testament are part of this revelation about Jesus.

Does that seem unlikely? And how does it work? I want to spend some time looking at parts of the Old Testament that are blamed for endorsing 'blatant misogyny' towards women. I want us to look head-on at those difficult parts and consider what these stories teach us. We can't ignore these things because they raise real concerns that God values women less than men, and therefore that God is not good.

---

3   2 Timothy 3:15-17

4   John 5:39

I am going start with the story of Tamar. She is not well known. Her history is hidden in the more well-known one of Joseph – of *Technicolour Dreamcoat* fame. Unsurprisingly she does not feature in Andrew Lloyd Webber's musical. Hers is one of those 'unpalatable' bits of the Bible which seems out of place in the middle of Joseph's story. So why does she feature? Why did she matter? Let's read her story. It begins like this:

At that time, Judah left his brothers and went down to stay with a man of Adullam named Hirah. There Judah met the daughter of a Canaanite man named Shua. He married her and made love to her; she became pregnant and gave birth to a son, who was named Er. She conceived again and gave birth to a son and named him Onan. She gave birth to still another son and named him Shelah. It was at Kezib that she gave birth to him.

Judah got a wife for Er, his firstborn, and her name was Tamar. But Er, Judah's firstborn, was wicked in the Lord's sight; so the Lord put him to death.

Then Judah said to Onan, 'Sleep with your brother's wife and fulfil your duty to her as a brother-in-law to raise up offspring for your brother.' But Onan knew that the child would not be his; so whenever he slept with his brother's wife, he spilled his semen on the ground to avoid providing offspring for his brother. What he did was wicked in the Lord's sight; so the Lord put him to death also.

Judah then said to his daughter-in-law Tamar, 'Live as a widow in your father's household until my son Shelah grows

*up.' For he thought, 'He may die too, just like his brothers.' So
Tamar went to live in her father's household.*[5]

These brief paragraphs cover about twenty-two years of
heartbreak. Can you imagine living through this? Tamar
experienced widowhood not once but twice followed by years
of neglect. Judah had gone against his family by marrying a
Canaanite woman. Rejecting his heritage was foolish. Judah's
family had been given an incredible inheritance. The Lord
had told his great-grandfather Abraham, that He would give
him many descendants, and a land. He had been promised a
relationship with God that would be a blessing to all peoples.
But Judah was not sticking around the family of promise;
he left to get married. But this is not a romantic story; the
language used to describe his marriage is crude. Sometimes
our modern versions of the Bible avoid the coarseness of the
original word, and this is one of those times. The Hebrew
doesn't say 'he married her and made love to her'; instead it
says: 'he took her'. This suggests force, and coercion, not a
whirlwind romance. The narrator doesn't elaborate on the
quality of this marriage. We do, however, get to know the
quality of the offspring.

Judah's sons were not good, in fact Er was so wicked that
the Lord put him to death. How evil must that have been? Er
came from a family with a poor track record. His father, Judah,
had rejected his family and married a Canaanite against their
will. His grandfather, Jacob, deceived his great-grandfather

---

5   Genesis 38:1-11

and cheated his brother out of his inheritance.[6] His father and uncles had plotted to kill their brother and then sold him to slavers. They had lied to their father and told him that his beloved son was dead.[7] When his aunt was raped, his uncles in retribution slaughtered the perpetrator along with all the men of his town. They then captured all the women and children and plundered everything.[8] How evil must Er have been? This is the first time in the Bible that it is stated explicitly that the Lord put that individual to death. How awful for Tamar to be married to him! How much choice do you think she had in the arrangement? Judah 'took' a wife for Er. It is hard to imagine that her experience of marriage was good.

But then things got worse for Tamar. Onan refused to take responsibility for his brother's wife. The custom of a brother marrying his brother's widow is difficult for us culturally, but it provided a way for the dead son to pass on his name and for the widow to be protected. This custom became enshrined in Jewish law many years later. However, Onan didn't want to provide an heir for his brother but was happy to sleep with Tamar. Regularly! How awful that must have been for her! The Lord put him to death too.

Tamar had one hope: to wait for Judah's youngest son to grow up. Meanwhile, Judah rejected her from his household. He shifted the responsibility for her protection and well-being back to her father. Tamar was vulnerable, her status was unclear. Judah had no intention of coming back for her,

6   Genesis 27
7   Genesis 37:12-36
8   Genesis 34

but she was not free to marry anyone else. When her father died, Tamar would be alone without any support. She was full of fear about her future. If you have ever read or watched a film version of *Pride and Prejudice* by Jane Austen, you will remember how paranoid Mrs Bennett was about her daughters remaining unmarried after their father's death. Women through the centuries and in many societies, needed marriage for financial security. Tamar was in no position to set herself up independently. So when all hope was lost she decided to take matters into her own hands:

After a long time Judah's wife, the daughter of Shua, died. When Judah had recovered from his grief, he went up to Timnah, to the men who were shearing his sheep, and his friend Hirah the Adullamite went with him.

When Tamar was told, 'Your father-in-law is on his way to Timnah to shear his sheep,' she took off her widow's clothes, covered herself with a veil to disguise herself, and then sat down at the entrance to Enaim, which is on the road to Timnah. For she saw that, though Shelah had now grown up, she had not been given to him as his wife.

When Judah saw her, he thought she was a prostitute, for she had covered her face. Not realising that she was his daughter-in-law, he went over to her by the roadside and said, 'Come now, let me sleep with you.'

'And what will you give me to sleep with you?' she asked.

'I'll send you a young goat from my flock,' he said.

'Will you give me something as a pledge until you send it?' she asked.

He said, 'What pledge should I give you?'

'Your seal and its cord, and the staff in your hand,' she answered. So he gave them to her and slept with her, and she became pregnant by him. After she left, she took off her veil and put on her widow's clothes again.

Meanwhile Judah sent the young goat by his friend the Adullamite in order to get his pledge back from the woman, but he did not find her. He asked the men who lived there, 'Where is the shrine-prostitute who was beside the road at Enaim?'

'There hasn't been any shrine-prostitute here,' they said.

So he went back to Judah and said, 'I didn't find her. Besides, the men who lived there said, "There hasn't been any shrine-prostitute here."'

Then Judah said, 'Let her keep what she has, or we will become a laughing-stock. After all, I did send her this young goat, but you didn't find her.'

About three months later Judah was told, 'Your daughter-in-law Tamar is guilty of prostitution, and as a result she is now pregnant.'

Judah said, 'Bring her out and let her be burned to death!'

As she was being brought out, she sent a message to her father-in-law. 'I am pregnant by the man who owns these,' she said. And she added, 'See if you recognise whose seal and cord and staff these are.'

Judah recognised them and said, 'She is more righteous than I, since I wouldn't give her to my son Shelah.' And he did not sleep with her again.

When the time came for her to give birth, there were twin boys in her womb. As she was giving birth, one of them put out his hand; so the midwife took a scarlet thread and tied it on his wrist and said, 'This one came out first.' But when he drew back his hand, his brother came out, and she said, 'So this is how you have broken out!' And he was named Perez. Then his brother, who had the scarlet thread on his wrist, came out. And he was named Zerah.[9]

In her desperation, Tamar planned for her father-in-law to father her child. This sounds awful to us but it wasn't out of line with the accepted ethical practices of the Hittite tradition. For it to work she needed Judah to sleep with her while she was disguised as a prostitute. Tamar had no doubt that he would sleep with a prostitute, which tells us all we need to know about Judah. She was right. She took Judah's seal and cord as a deposit for payment and as proof of his identity. After sleeping with him she dressed again in her widow's clothes. Judah did try to pay her but he gave up quite quickly when she couldn't be found. He was a proud man who didn't want it to be known that a prostitute had tricked him out of his means of identifying himself. However, when Tamar's pregnancy was discovered, Judah was far from quiet. He wanted Tamar publicly shamed and executed. His sentence was chilling: *'bring her out and let her be burned to death'.*

---

9   Genesis 38:12-30

It is hard to conceive that Judah believed that this was just. It is hypocrisy at its ugliest. He slept with prostitutes, but his daughter-in-law could be burned to death for being a prostitute. This is not ok! The writer of this story is exposing Judah, not commending him. Later on in the Old Testament, the prophet Hosea is explicit about not condemning women for their sexual behaviour while letting men off:

I will not punish your daughters
   when they turn to prostitution,
nor your daughters-in-law
   when they commit adultery,
because the men themselves consort with harlots
   and sacrifice with shrine-prostitutes –
   a people without understanding will come to ruin![10]

Judah's quick sentencing of Tamar is murderous. Her death would have been convenient for him. It would have freed him of his responsibility to a woman he considered a bad omen. Fortunately, Tamar had foreseen this. The seal and cord she had asked for enabled her to unmask Judah's failure and hypocrisy. The man who was afraid of losing face was laid bare and humiliated. Tamar was reprieved and exonerated. It is a sordid tale which ends with a happy ever after of sorts for Tamar. She was finally brought into the protection of Judah's family without the humiliation of having to sleep with Judah again. Finally, she gave birth to not one child but two, a double blessing for the childless Tamar.

---

10   Hosea 4:14

Why are these messy lives recorded as part of the Bible story? Firstly, the Bible is realistic about people: it does not romanticise its heroes, and it is honest about the difficulties women have faced. When you think about it, it's remarkable that this story is here at all. This sort of sordid family story is usually kept a secret, a skeleton in the cupboard, even more so when the family is established and influential. You can imagine the hushed whispers and rumours concerning the parentage of the twins. But this was not only passed on; it was considered important enough to be recorded in Israel's books of the law. This is because it serves as a witness to the transformation that took place in Judah's life. He changed from fearing being a laughing stock to publicly acknowledging his sin: *'She is more righteous than I, since I wouldn't give her to my son Shelah.'* This marked the beginning of a massive change for Judah. He went back to his father and committed himself to his family. Later on, he was the one who would take responsibility for his brother Benjamin's safety in Egypt.[11] He kept this promise to the point of offering himself as a slave in his brother's place.[12] If only Andrew Lloyd Webber had understood the dramatic impact of the moment Judah stepped up to protect Benjamin. Joseph saw it. It reduced him to tears and moved him to reveal himself to his brothers.[13] Judah's encounter with Tamar humbled him and changed him. Moreover, his story did not end there. His father, Jacob, gave him a place of honour in the

---

11   Genesis 43: 2-9

12   Genesis 44:33-34

13   Genesis 45

family and a blessing like none of his other brothers. The once rebellious Judah received an incredible promise:

> *The sceptre will not depart from Judah,*
>   *nor the ruler's staff from between his feet,*
> *until he to whom it belongs shall come*
>   *and the obedience of the nations shall be his.*[14]

Sinful Judah, who was brought to his senses by Tamar, was told that through his family line God would bring one who would become the ruler of the whole world. So is this a man's story after all? What about Tamar? What happens to her story?

When Judah said Tamar is more righteous than I, he was not suggesting she was perfect, but he is admitting she is a lot better than him. Tamar was doing what she could for survival. She was an unlikely candidate, a Canaanite woman, yet she became fully incorporated into God's people with not just one son but two, neither of whom were treated as illegitimate. Despite her background, she was brought into the promised family of Abraham. Tamar, who was neglected and rejected, became part of the royal family line which God was establishing. Her offspring mattered. She mattered. Her story was told. Tamar's action ensured that despite Onan's repeated spilling of seed Judah would have offspring, an offspring that would be part of a royal line as recorded in the book of Ruth. This act was recorded so well that it became part of a traditional blessing:

---

14 Genesis 49:10

> *Then the elders and all the people at the gate said, 'We are witnesses. May the Lord make the woman who is coming into your home like Rachel and Leah, who together built up the family of Israel. May you have standing in Ephrathah and be famous in Bethlehem. Through the offspring the Lord gives you by this young woman, may your family be like that of Perez, whom Tamar bore to Judah.'*[15]

Tamar was celebrated. The woman who thought she would have no family had a son whose family line led to Israel's greatest kings:

> *This, then, is the family line of Perez:*
> *Perez was the father of Hezron,*
> *Hezron the father of Ram,*
> *Ram the father of Amminadab,*
> *Amminadab the father of Nahshon,*
> *Nahshon the father of Salmon,[d]*
> *Salmon the father of Boaz,*
> *Boaz the father of Obed,*
> *Obed the father of Jesse,*
> *and Jesse the father of David.*[16]

Tamar's son is the ancestor of a greater son, David, who was the great king of Israel. This family line extends to the greatest king and Tamar even gets acknowledgement in the beginning of the gospel of Matthew:

> *This is the genealogy of Jesus the Messiah, the son of David, the son of Abraham:*

15 Ruth 4:11-12

16 Ruth 4:18-22

Abraham was the father of Isaac,
Isaac the father of Jacob,
Jacob the father of Judah and his brothers,
Judah the father of Perez and Zerah, whose mother was
Tamar.[17]

Of all the women to mention in the genealogy of Jesus, Matthew name-drops Tamar. She is there in the list of names that point to God's great rescue plan fulfilled by Jesus Christ. Jesus, the ultimate offspring who came to defeat evil, the one who was promised in Genesis 3:15. He was the one bruised when He was put to death on the cross, but who crushed Satan's power as He died.

I rejoice in this story. It shows how God draws unlikely and broken people into His family. No one is too bad to be brought in: even Judah could be rescued. The promise of God is available to all. I don't know where you place yourself regarding God. You may consider yourself well-rounded, with life sorted out and in no need of God's rescue in Jesus. Indeed, in comparison to Judah, you probably look really good. But the truth is that no one is right with God, not one of us is 'righteous'. We are mistaken if we think God will be pleased with us because we live according to our own standards of goodness, because even the best of us are not truly good. It is not 'good' people that God brings into His family. C.S. Lewis put it like this:

The Christian does not think that God will love us because we are good, but that God will make us good because He loves us;

---

17   Matthew 1:1-3

just as the roof of a greenhouse does not attract the sun because it is bright, but becomes bright because the sun shines on it.[18]

We all come with mess, men and women alike. But God's nature is to rescue messy people; people like Judah and Tamar. God saves people like us. Right at the beginning of the Bible story, we see God's heart as He brings into His family all types of broken and vulnerable people while transforming the rebellious and self-centred. Genesis explains how everything went wrong but gives us a glimpse of how God will put everything right despite the evil in the world. The joy of Genesis is that despite the fall, God works out His rescue plan and nothing, especially human broken relationships and sinfulness, will stop it. God can change people.

We need to know this! We can feel overwhelmed by the evil we experience, the horrors we hear via the news, or on our Twitter feeds. Sometimes it seems evil wins all the time, but that's not true. God is not defeated by sin. The story of Tamar interwoven in Joseph's story makes this point; despite sinfulness, God was working out His saving plan. At the end of his life, Joseph learned the same thing. He said to his brothers:

You intended to harm me, but God intended it for good to accomplish what is now being done, the saving of many lives.[19]

Centuries later, we see this truth magnified in the terrible act of crucifying God's own Son, the promised offspring; yet through Jesus' death, God was saving many lives. Humanity's

---

18   C.S. Lewis, *Mere Christianity*, p. 61

19   Genesis 50:20

worst acts do not throw God off course. God can use evil to bring about good.

Tamar's story gives us great hope. It is one of the more 'palatable' stories after all. But not all the stories in the Bible end this well. Turn the page with me because we need to look at possibly the darkest episode of all.

For Further Thought and Conversation

- Do you think that the Bible is full of 'blatant misogyny and barbarity towards women'?
- What bits are you thinking of?
- Why do you think the Bible was written?
- What do you make of Paul's explanation?

Read Genesis 38

- How do you feel about Judah?
- How do you feel about Tamar?
- What do you make of Tamar being included in the genealogy of Jesus?
- What does this story teach us about the nature of God?

7 FROM BAD TO WORSE

On the 16th of December 2012, a crime took place that shocked the world. It sparked a wave of public protests, and the United Nations Secretary-General Ban Ki-moon made a statement: 'Violence against women must never be accepted, never excused, never tolerated. Every girl and woman has the right to be respected, valued, and protected.'[1]

A young woman in South Delhi had been to see a film with a male friend. Around 9pm in the evening they boarded a bus for home. There were six other passengers on the bus. What happened next was terrifying. They both were attacked; the young woman raped by all six passengers and the bus driver. This was the kind of rape that cannot be imagined. When she fought back, she was abused more. One of her attackers later said she died because she had not submitted to her attackers: 'She should just be silent and allow the rape. Then they'd have

---

1   Manash Pratim Gohain, TNN (31 December 2012). 'Ban expresses condolences on death of gang-rape victim, urges reforms to deter violence against women'. *The Times of India*. Retrieved 29 June 2013.

dropped her off after doing her and only hit the boy.'[2] But she did fight back. She died of her injuries on the 29th December 2012.

In India, to protect rape victims, they are not named publicly. The media called this young woman, 'Nirbhaya', which means fearless one. However, shortly after her death, her father told the world's media that he wanted his daughter's real name to be known because she had done nothing wrong and he was proud of her.[3] He announced to the world that her name was Jyoti Singh Pandey. Jyoti means light. Her father said in a BBC documentary:

> *She has become a symbol of women's empowerment. She has lit a flame, and we have to keep that flame burning.*[4]

Since her death, there have been changes in the legal system in India, including the introduction of a mandatory term of twenty years for gang rape. Over the years, there have been others who suffered like Jyoti, some whose names no one knows; silent victims, who never received justice. The brutal murder and rape of women has been a dark and constant undercurrent; there is no country untouched by this horrendous crime. Jyoti lit a flame in India.

---

2 http://www.independent.co.uk/news/world/asia/delhi-bus-rapist-blames-dead-victim-for-attack-because-girls-are-responsible-for-rape-10079894.html Last accessed May 2021

3 https://www.washingtonpost.com/blogs/she-the-people/wp/2013/01/07/father-of-new-delhi-rape-victim-tell-the-world-my-daughters-name/ Last accessed May 2021

4 BBC documentary *Storyville: India's Daughter* (March 2015). Directed by Leslee Udwin

There is another woman whose flame still burns through the centuries. Her name is known only to God, but her plight continues to move us to tears and demands justice. Her story is recorded in the Old Testament book of Judges. It is brutal:

> Now a Levite who lived in a remote area in the hill country of Ephraim took a concubine from Bethlehem in Judah. But she was unfaithful to him. She left him and went back to her parents' home in Bethlehem, Judah. After she had been there for four months, her husband went to her to persuade her to return. He had with him his servant and two donkeys. She took him into her parents' home, and when her father saw him, he gladly welcomed him. His father-in-law, the woman's father, prevailed on him to stay; so he remained with him three days, eating and drinking, and sleeping there.
>
> On the fourth day they got up early and he prepared to leave, but the woman's father said to his son-in-law, 'Refresh yourself with something to eat; then you can go.' So the two of them sat down to eat and drink together. Afterwards the woman's father said, 'Please stay tonight and enjoy yourself.' And when the man got up to go, his father-in-law persuaded him, so he stayed there that night. On the morning of the fifth day, when he rose to go, the woman's father said, 'Refresh yourself. Wait till afternoon!' So the two of them ate together.
>
> Then when the man, with his concubine and his servant, got up to leave, his father-in-law, the woman's father, said, 'Now look, it's almost evening. Spend the night here; the day is nearly over. Stay and enjoy yourself. Early tomorrow morning you can get up and be on your way home.' But, unwilling to stay another

night, the man left and went towards Jebus (that is, Jerusalem), with his two saddled donkeys and his concubine.[5]

This starts as a domestic story centred on an unnamed Levite. This means he belonged to the priestly tribe of Israel, which had spiritual responsibility for the nation. This spiritual leader had taken a concubine, a practice that was not promoted in the law. A concubine referred to a secondary or inferior wife or sometimes to a slave girl who bore children.[6] We don't know much about this particular arrangement, but it is noticeable that the concubine's father was described by the title 'father-in-law' and her husband as 'son-in-law'.[7] However, the relationship between this man and his concubine was troubled. She had returned to her father's house, and her husband had gone to get her back. We are told that she had been unfaithful to him. The Hebrew word used here is *'zanah'*, which has sometimes been translated as she 'played the whore against him'. However, more recent scholarship has shown that it can also mean 'to be angry, hateful' or to 'feel repugnant against'.[8] It seems then that the concubine had fallen out with her husband and was angry with him, for what reason we do not know. It is unlikely that she had been involved in prostitution because her father welcomed her and her husband travelled to

5   Judges 19:1-10

6   Richard M. Davidson, *Flame of Yahweh: Sexuality in the Old Testament* (Baker Academic, 2007), p. 186

7   Paul Copan, *Is God a Moral Monster? Making Sense of the Old Testament God* (BakerBooks, 2011), p. 111

8   https://claudemariottini.com/2006/01/06/rereading-judges-192/ accessed February 2017

persuade her to come back to him. The Levite was successful, and despite reluctance on her father's part, the arrangement was made for her to return. It proved fatal:

When they were near Jebus and the day was almost gone, the servant said to his master, 'Come, let's stop at this city of the Jebusites and spend the night.'

His master replied, 'No. We won't go into any city whose people are not Israelites. We will go on to Gibeah.' He added, 'Come, let's try to reach Gibeah or Ramah and spend the night in one of those places.' So they went on, and the sun set as they neared Gibeah in Benjamin. There they stopped to spend the night. They went and sat in the city square, but no one took them in for the night.

That evening an old man from the hill country of Ephraim, who was living in Gibeah (the inhabitants of the place were Benjaminites), came in from his work in the fields. When he looked and saw the traveller in the city square, the old man asked, 'Where are you going? Where did you come from?'

He answered, 'We are on our way from Bethlehem in Judah to a remote area in the hill country of Ephraim where I live. I have been to Bethlehem in Judah and now I am going to the house of the Lord. No one has taken me in for the night. We have both straw and fodder for our donkeys and bread and wine for ourselves your servants – me, the woman and the young man with us. We don't need anything.'

'You are welcome at my house,' the old man said. 'Let me supply whatever you need. Only don't spend the night in the square.' So

he took him into his house and fed his donkeys. After they had washed their feet, they had something to eat and drink.[9]

The party had left it far too late to complete their journey in one day but decided to travel anyway. The Levite didn't consider it safe to stop overnight in the foreign territory of Jebus; instead, he headed for the Israelite town of Gibeah. This was a mistake; things were not as they should be in Gibeah. No one offered them hospitality, the usual custom, and it looked like they would have to sleep out in the open. Finally, they were welcomed into an old man's home who said with a sense of foreboding: 'Don't spend the night in the square'. Nevertheless, the Levite and his concubine must have felt safe as they washed from their journey and sat down to eat. After all, the concubine was in the protection of her husband and enjoying the hospitality of an Israelite in an Israelite town, yet she was far from safe:

While they were enjoying themselves, some of the wicked men of the city surrounded the house. Pounding on the door, they shouted to the old man who owned the house, 'Bring out the man who came to your house so we can have sex with him.'

The owner of the house went outside and said to them, 'No, my friends, don't be so vile. Since this man is my guest, don't do this outrageous thing. Look, here is my virgin daughter, and his concubine. I will bring them out to you now, and you can use them and do to them whatever you wish. But as for this man, don't do such an outrageous thing.'

---

9   Judges 19:11-21

But the men would not listen to him. So the man took his concubine and sent her outside to them, and they raped her and abused her throughout the night, and at dawn they let her go. At daybreak the woman went back to the house where her master was staying, fell down at the door and lay there until daylight.

When her master got up in the morning and opened the door of the house and stepped out to continue on his way, there lay his concubine, fallen in the doorway of the house, with her hands on the threshold. He said to her, 'Get up; let's go.' But there was no answer. Then the man put her on his donkey and set out for home.

When he reached home, he took a knife and cut up his concubine, limb by limb, into twelve parts and sent them into all the areas of Israel. Everyone who saw it was saying to one another, 'Such a thing has never been seen or done, not since the day the Israelites came up out of Egypt. Just imagine! We must do something! So speak up!'[10]

This is harrowing to read; the threat escalates with wave upon wave of horror. The men of the town first demand sex with the Levite which the old man sees as abhorrent. He refuses their request but has no such hesitation offering the women, including his own daughter. The women are expendable. The Levite shields his host's daughter but does not guard his concubine. This was the woman he travelled to retrieve, the one whose father had reluctantly entrusted to him. He thrust her out to face a violent gang of men, vulnerable and alone. What happened to her is not recorded in detail; this says it all:

10   Judges 19:22-30

'they raped her and abused her.' We know what that means, we know the hideous acts referred to. It killed her. How old was she? We don't know. Her life was snatched away by a ruthless and foul mob: a victim of her society, and of the man who had a responsibility to care for her. She was failed at every point.

Why does the Bible describe such ugliness? Not because God approves of it. This story is not prescriptive but descriptive. It isn't there to show us how to live but how we do live. It is here because God doesn't hide from us the depths of savagery we are capable of. We may want to close our eyes and ears to this woman's cries, but God wants us to see and understand. What happened to this woman is a reflection of what has happened to other young women. It is what happened to Jyoti, and it matters.

In 2010, a film was released called *The Whistleblower*. It told the true story of Kathryn Bolkovac working in Bosnia as a United Nations International Police Force Monitor. She lost her job for whistleblowing about the sex trafficking of women. This trade had been going on among and by those who had been charged with establishing peace. The women were enslaved, treated appallingly, and their rights disregarded. Their voices were dismissed because they were considered: 'whores of war'. Miroslav Volf, a Croatian theologian, who saw first hand the violence in the Balkans, reached this conclusion: 'if God were not angry at injustice and deception and did not make a final end to violence – that God would not be worthy of worship.'[11]

---

11   Quoted in Timothy Keller, *The Reason for God* (Hodder & Stoughton, 2008) p. 74

Volf is right; God is angry at humanity's savagery. The Bible rejoices that one day, He will destroy evil:

> *After this I heard what sounded like the roar of a great*
> *multitude in heaven shouting:*
> *'Hallelujah!*
> *Salvation and glory and power belong to our God,*
> *   for true and just are his judgments.*
> *He has condemned the great prostitute*
> *   who corrupted the earth by her adulteries.*
> *He has avenged on her the blood of his servants.'*[12]

We can feel uncomfortable with the idea of a final judgement. But we need it. We need God to judge. Our attempts at justice are inadequate. Miroslav Volf argues that it is only God we can fully trust to bring righteous justice. When we try to sort it out ourselves, we often go far beyond justice into vengeance.[13] The Levite wanted revenge. In his rage, he mutilated his concubine's body and sent her body parts to all of the tribes in Israel. His response was a gruesome call to arms: 'We must do something! So speak up!' He was determined that somebody should punish those who did it. He was right; it is a crime that shouts out for justice. The chapters that follow show Israel was incapable of bringing it. The death of the Levite's concubine resulted in a bloody civil war in which thousands were killed.[14]

---

12   Revelation 19:1-2

13   Miroslav Volf, *Exclusion and Embrace: A Theological Exploration of Identity, Otherness, and Reconciliation* (Abingdon Press, 1996), pp. 303-304

14   Judges 20

These terrible events show the destructive degradation of humanity. The account began with these words: 'In those days Israel had no king,' and the book of Judges ends with: 'In those days Israel had no king; everyone did as they saw fit.'[15] Yet Israel did have a king, not a human ruler but God who is the ruler of the world. He had given them clear directions about the right way to live. The shock for the original hearers is not only what happened to the concubine, but that this horror took place in Israel, in their community! There was depravity at the heart of Israel even though God had given them so much. This was the nation that had been called to live differently from others around them. They had been given the law to help them have a relationship with God and each other. Despite all of this, they failed. It was not a small failure; it was catastrophic.

The Israelites had been so sure that they were the 'goodies': after all, they were God's chosen people who had a special relationship with Him. The Levite wouldn't stay in a Gentile city; he didn't trust foreigners; they were the 'baddies'. Now it was clear that even Israel lived without regard to God. They also were ruled by their passions and desires and lived as they saw fit. They too were evil. The book of Judges doesn't show us the cruelty of God; instead, it shines a spotlight on the evil that results when people live without regard to God. Abuse doesn't originate from God but is a consequence when humanity lives without God as their King.

God didn't step in to rescue the Levite's concubine. Her name is not even recorded. Nevertheless, that does not mean

---

15   Judges 21:25

she didn't matter to God. He saw. He continues to see the brutality young girls and women face. He knows about the abuse of refugees fleeing war and poverty. We see it and cry out with hopelessness. Why doesn't He intervene? The prophets in the past cried out: 'How long? Is God good? Can we trust Him?'[16] We long to see justice done and it will be; God cares, He hates evil. He weeps with us at the heinous nature of sin. He understands it better than we do. He sees it all. He hears our cries for justice. He knows it must be punished and promises to do it. One day through Christ, every evil act will be brought to account; every anonymous victim will know that the evil perpetrated towards them mattered. There will be an end:

> *This will take place on the day when God judges people's secrets through Jesus Christ, as my gospel declares.*[17]

In October 2016 Columbia had a peace referendum following fighting of many years between the government forces and FARC[18] rebels. The FARC rebels had committed numerous acts of killing, kidnapping, and child recruitment for their army. They had subjected young girls to rape, sterilisation, forced abortion, and other forms of sexual violence. The terms of the proposed peace deal were laid out in a referendum which would have allowed the rebel leaders to avoid jail. Although the country was desperate for peace, voters couldn't stomach the idea that past crimes would be ignored. It was reported

---

16   see Habakkuk 1:1-4

17   Romans 2:16

18   FARC – the revolutionary forces of Columbia

that 'No' voters wanted FARC commanders to face prison, be banned from Congress and to give back land and money.[19] Justice matters, evil cannot be swept under the carpet. We long for it with all of our beings. We need it.

The problem with the judgement of God, however, is that although we can agree that some acts are evil and deserve punishment, other things we consider less serious. It is hard to acknowledge our own guilt. We like to think that our sin is different and doesn't matter as much. C.S. Lewis described it like this:

> We have a strange illusion that mere time cancels sin. I have heard others, and I have heard myself, recounting cruelties and falsehoods committed in boyhood as if they were no concern of the present speaker's, and even with laughter. But mere time does nothing either to the fact or to the guilt of a sin. The guilt is washed out not by time but by repentance and the blood of Christ: if we have repented these early sins we should remember the price of our forgiveness and be humble.[20]

I wonder how you see yourself. I find it an uncomfortable thought standing before Christ, the judge of the living and the dead and imagining my every secret thought, my motives, my desires, and my actions all laid bare. I consider myself respectable, not perfect, but not as bad as abusers, rapists, and criminals. But although I can congratulate myself for not being as bad as I could be, before our perfectly holy God, I know I

---

19 http://www.aljazeera.com/indepth/opinion/2016/10/colombians-opposed-peace-deal-farc-161004064506763.html accessed February 2017

20 C.S. Lewis, *The Problem of Pain* (1940), (Collins, 2012) p. 54

am not as good as I should be. Before God, we are all exposed. He knows our secret hatreds, our selfish ambitions, our cruel remarks, our lack of love, our laziness, our self-centredness, and our callous indifference. Before God, I cannot stand; no one can stand. Before God, I will know I deserve judgement too.

This is a serious problem. We need justice from a good judge, but that means we too must be judged and we are also guilty. We need forgiveness from this righteous judge, but how can God forgive us without ignoring our sin? How can God say we are right when we are wrong without becoming an unjust judge? This is the reason for the cross. God resolved this central dilemma through Jesus, who is both Saviour and judge. Jesus is the rescuer who experienced God's righteous anger and was punished on the cross in our place even though He was innocent. He knew the capacity of our sinful hearts yet willingly died for us. Jesus knew that sin mattered; He could not just 'forgive and forget' but He wanted to restore us. To free us from the depths of our depravity He gave everything He had:

> He himself bore our sins in his body on the cross, so that we might die to sins and live for righteousness; by his wounds you have been healed.[21]

Jesus gave more than anyone possibly could give. It is possible to die for someone else, but no one else could take the punishment we deserve:

---

21 1 Peter 2:24

You see, at just the right time, when we were still powerless, Christ died for the ungodly. Very rarely will anyone die for a righteous person, though for a good person someone might possibly dare to die. But God demonstrates his own love for us in this: while we were still sinners, Christ died for us.[22]

It is amazing love. There is a hymn that puts it like this:

This is amazing grace
This is unfailing love
That You would take my place
That You would bear my cross
You lay down Your life
That I would be set free
Oh, Jesus, I sing for
All that You've done for me.[23]

This is remarkable, it is amazing grace. God provides us with more justice than we can ever contemplate and more grace than we could ever deserve. It is very good news for us all.

FOR FURTHER THOUGHT AND CONVERSATION

Violence against women must never be accepted, never excused, never tolerated. Every girl and woman has the right to be respected, valued, and protected.[24]

- What would you do to achieve this?
- What changes do you think we need to protect women in our society?

22 Romans 5:6-8

23 Phil Wickham, 'This is Amazing Grace'

24 Ban Ki-moon, United Nations Secretary-General

- Where do you think abuse originates?
- In cases of violence against women, what does justice look like to you?
- Why do we find it hard to achieve justice?

Read Romans 2:5-16

- What is the basis of God's judgement?
- How do you feel about God judging your life?
- How can God forgive anyone, justly? (Read Rom. 3:21-27)

8 WORRYING LAWS

In the previous chapter, we saw that the abuse of women does not originate from God, but people living without regard to God as their acknowledged King. But is this strictly true? Aren't there parts of the Bible where we find God advocating terrible attitudes to women? What about those texts which describe God's commands to Israel? Aren't parts of the law hostile towards women? David described the law as: *'Perfect, refreshing the soul. The statutes of the Lord are trustworthy, making wise the simple.'*[1] But some can read the law and find things in it that are far from refreshing. The law that originates with God and reflects His nature they see as sexist and misogynistic. They suspect it teaches that women are the property of men; that women are singled out for cruel punishment and viewed as dishonourable and unclean. They believe that the law is all about restriction and not about flourishing.

---

1   Psalm 19:7

So how should we view the law? Israel was given the law after they were rescued from Egypt; it contained special instructions to establish them as God's set-apart people.[2] Israel bound themselves to it in a covenant.[3] We need to bear in mind that this law is no longer binding, as Paul Copan says:

Keep in mind this statement that is worthy of full acceptance: the law of Moses is not eternal and unchanging.[4]

As the Old Testament story unfolds, the prophets pointed towards the day when God would change everything.[5] Jesus fulfilled the law[6] perfectly and established a new covenant.[7] However, when God gave Israel the law it provided a way for them to live together as a newly formed nation as God's people. This law had a radically different structure from the societies around them:

Israel had a tribal and kinship structure. Economic, judicial, religious, and even military aspects of life were oriented around this social formation. By contrast, Canaanites had a kind of feudal system with a powerful elite at the top and peasants at the bottom.[8]

---

2   Exodus 19:1-6

3   Exodus 24:1-11

4   Copan, *Is God a Moral Monster?*, p. 71

5   Jeremiah 31:31

6   Matthew 5:17-18

7   Luke 22:20

8   Copan, *Is God a Moral Monster?*, p. 70

Women in these ancient cultures were particularly vulnerable. In societies where the physically powerful ruled the roost, women were at risk without the support of their families. We have already seen the precariousness of Tamar's situation. Israel's law was designed to care for the vulnerable with particular regard for those without a family: the widows, the orphans, and the outsiders. God's compassion for the weak pulses through the law:

> *If any of your fellow Israelites become poor and are unable to support themselves among you, help them as you would a foreigner and stranger, so that they can continue to live among you.*[9]

> *He defends the cause of the fatherless and the widow, and loves the foreigner residing among you, giving them food and clothing.*[10]

The law that God gave to Israel was to be protective. It forbade practices such as child sacrifice which was known in the surrounding cultures. God hated child sacrifice.

> *Do not give any of your children to be sacrificed to Molek, for you must not profane the name of your God. I am the Lord.*[11]

Human sacrifice was and is abhorrent to God. It is never OK. One of the judges, Jephthah, made a foolish vow to sacrifice whoever came out to meet him following his victory

---

9   Leviticus 25:35

10   Deuteronomy 10:18

11   Leviticus 18:21

in battle.[12] This passage is sometimes read as an example of human sacrifice, but this is highly unlikely. The threat in the narrative is not of death but a life of singleness. The story emphasises that it was his only child that meets Jephthah. She asks to mourn not her impending death but the prospect of not marrying. The issue at stake in this story is enforced virginity and the absence of descendants: a considerable loss for Jephthah's family.[13] Jephthah's vow was wrong, but he is not being accused of murdering his daughter.

There is no denying that Israel was a patriarchal society. A feminist understanding of patriarchy is that patriarchy is at its core an abusive system. Sylvia Walby describes it as: 'a system of interrelated social structures which allow men to exploit women.'[14] She argues that patriarchy is a system that brings tension and conflict rather than an order of harmony and mutual accommodation. But is this fair? No, in the law, God provided a protective framework for the whole of Israelite society that had the potential for harmony, as Paul Copan observes:

In Israel's legislation, God does two things: (1) he works within a patriarchal society to point Israel to a better path; and (2) he

---

12   Judges 11:29-40

13   Judges 11. See Miles Van Pelt 'Rethinking Jephthah's Foolish vow' https://www.thegospelcoalition.org/article/rethinking-jephthah-foolish-vow/ Last accessed May 2021

14   Sylvia Walby, *Patriarchy at Work* (Minneapolis: University of Minnesota Press, 1986), p. 51

provides many protections and controls against abuses directed at females ...[15]

Rather than Israelite women being viewed as second-class citizens, they were given unusually high status, in comparison to women in the surrounding cultures. Carol Meyers argues that:

The husband's formal 'authority' is balanced by the domestic-orientated 'power' in the hands of the wife and mother of the Israelite household, if ever there were a situation in which the condescending phrase 'only a wife and mother' should be expunged from descriptive language, the family household of early Israel should surely qualify.[16]

The status of women in Israel is seen in the fact that mothers are named alongside fathers in the ten commandments:

Honour your father and your mother, so that you may live long in the land the Lord your God is giving you.[17]

When this command was repeated later the order changes so that the mother is the first-named member of the household: *'Each of you must respect your* mother *and father.'[18]* A mother was never under the authority of her sons, unlike other ancient and not so ancient societies:

In Saudi Arabia, a woman's life is controlled by a man from birth until death. Every Saudi woman must have a male

15   Copan, *Is God a Moral Monster?,* p.102

16   Davidson, *Flame of Yahweh,* p.220

17   Exodus 20:12

18   Leviticus 19:3

guardian, normally a father or husband, but in some cases a brother or even a son, who has the power to make a range of critical decisions on her behalf. As dozens of Saudi women told Human Rights Watch, the male guardianship system is the most significant impediment to realising women's rights in the country, effectively rendering adult women legal minors who cannot make key decisions for themselves.[19]

In 2019 Saudi Arabia began some reform of this system,[20] but at the time of writing, women are still widely restricted.[21] It seems that the ancient Israelite woman had more rights; in fact, a son could be punished for rebelling against his mother's authority. And as Tikva Frymer-Kensky observed: 'The power of the husband over the wife is not generalized to all men over all females.'[22] In Israel, women could exert influence and power over their households. There was one difference: the husband or father had legal responsibilities in some areas:

His leadership and legal authority are evidenced in such concerns as family inheritance and ownership of property, contracting marriages for the children, and overall responsibility in speaking for his family.[23]

---

19 https://www.hrw.org/report/2016/07/16/boxed/women-and-saudi-arabias-male-guardianship-system accessed 30 March 2017

20 https://www.theguardian.com/world/2019/jul/11/saudi-arabia-planning-to-relax-male-guardianship-laws accessed August 2019

21 https://www.equalitynow.org/ending_male_guardianship_in_saudi_arabia accessed October 2020

22 Quoted in Davidson, *Flame of Yahweh,* p. 222

23 Ibid. p. 215

The father was not allowed to exploit the women in his family. His role was to ensure a system of harmony and mutual accommodation for his household. The system that God gave to Israel was designed so that everyone in the ancient Israelite community might flourish.

There was equality in the law. Both men and women were to participate in the formal worship of the community. Both were called to obedience and punished for disobedience. Men and women were held equally accountable and responsible for sexual crimes. However, there are still some things that remain hard for us to get our heads around. Some areas which I grappled with were: the teaching on polygamy, rape, trials, and purification laws. Let's look at each one in turn.

Does God Permit Polygamy?

> *If a man has two wives, and he loves one but not the other, and both bear him sons but the firstborn is the son of the wife he does not love, when he wills his property to his sons, he must not give the rights of the firstborn to the son of the wife he loves in preference to his actual firstborn, the son of the wife he does not love. He must acknowledge the son of his unloved wife as the firstborn by giving him a double share of all he has. That son is the first sign of his father's strength. The right of the firstborn belongs to him.[24]*

Reading through the Old Testament, it is easy to think that God actively promotes polygamy. Many leading figures practised it in some form: Abraham, Jacob, David,

---

24   Deuteronomy 21:15-17

and Solomon; although in each case, it is clear that these relationships caused considerable difficulties. Biblical writers show the flaws of even the most renowned characters. As Paul Copan notes, these individuals' status was not because of their moral perfection but because of their uncompromising faith.[25] They required God's mercy and grace as much as the rest of us. They were men of their time. Polygamy did not come with God's stamp of approval. However, its practice was common in the ancient Near East, particularly if a man's first wife was presumed to be infertile or she became sick;[26] indeed, it was sanctioned in the Code of Hammurabi in these cases.[27] The Middle Assyrian Laws assumed polygamy as the norm, placing no limits on the practice or number of wives.[28] However, it was a practice in which women, in particular, suffered. The Bible describes the pain of both Hagar[29] and Hannah.[30] Polygamy also proved disastrous to men: David's complicated family situation brought much trouble in the latter part of his reign.[31] Whereas, Solomon's many marriages led him into idolatry which caused the eventual division of

---

25 Copan, *Is God a Moral Monster?*, p. 67

26 Ibid., p.110

27 Babylonian ancient law (141,145, 148) dating around 1754 BC, *The Code of Hammurabi*, translated by L.W. King, p. 48

28 Davidson, *Flame of Yahweh*, p. 179

29 Genesis 16

30 1 Samuel 1:1-7

31 2 Samuel 13–18

Israel.[32] Yet if it was so disastrous, why did God put a provision into the law concerning polygamous marriages?

I struggled with this until I realised that many of Israel's laws are case laws. Jesus Himself taught us how to understand case law. Jesus was asked by some critical Pharisees whether or not divorce was legal.[33] Technically divorce existed in the law. The Pharisees knew that Moses had put in a provision for a certificate of divorce.[34] Jesus, however, took them back to God's ideal for marriage, as described in Genesis 2. He then explained why the law on divorce existed:

> *'It was because your hearts were hard that Moses wrote you this law,' Jesus replied. 'But at the beginning of creation God "made them male and female". "For this reason a man will leave his father and mother and be united to his wife, and the two will become one flesh." So they are no longer two, but one flesh. Therefore what God has joined together, let no one separate.'*[35]

The law was given because their hearts were hard, not because God thought divorce was a great idea. This principle explains why much of the law was given: human sinfulness. God, in His goodness, provided for those that were vulnerable because of the sin of others. This is casuistic law. We have laws like this in our legal system. Similarly, the law regarding polygamy is case law given to protect the son of a first wife. It is not promoting polygamy but protecting those caught up in it from its worse

32 1 Kings 11

33 Mark 10:1-9

34 Deuteronomy 24:1-4

35 Mark 10:5-9

consequences. It established the principle that the son of the less-favoured wife could not be disregarded and deprived of their inheritance because of bad relationships and favouritism.

Does God Advocate Rape?

When you go to war against your enemies and the Lord your God delivers them into your hands and you take captives, if you notice among the captives a beautiful woman and are attracted to her, you may take her as your wife. Bring her into your home and make her shave her head, trim her nails and put aside the clothes she was wearing when captured. After she has lived in your house and mourned her father and mother for a full month, then you may go to her and be her husband and she shall be your wife. If you are not pleased with her, let her go wherever she wishes. You must not sell her or treat her as a slave, since you have dishonoured her.[36]

Violence and sexual abuse in war are well documented and remain a problem:

Rape and sexual violence used to be perceived as inevitable by-products of war, the spoils of an invading army or a successful conqueror. However, the international community now recognises that rape and sexual violence is often used as a deliberate military strategy to demoralise an enemy. This shift in recognition has been significant, especially as it has allowed for the prosecution of sexual violence in conflict.[37]

---

36   Deuteronomy 21:10-14

37   https://www.forbes.com/sites/ewelinaochab/2017/03/02/sexual-violence-as-a-weapon-of-war-the-story-of-daesh-and-boko-haram/#701fdcf96a17 accessed 31 March 2017

The rape of women in areas of conflict is a crime, so how can we reconcile a law that allows an Israelite soldier to take a woman that he was attracted to from among his captives? It appears to advocate the sexual abuse of a vulnerable young woman. Was God allowing abuse? If we read this carefully, we will see the opposite is the case. This is another example of case law. Kathleen Nielson explains:

> *God is not endorsing the taking of women captive; the context here is descriptive, not prescriptive. The capturing of women in war or in any context is sin, dreadful sin.*[38]

As a captive, the woman was in a terrible situation; a victim of war exiled from her home, bereaved, defenceless, and unsafe. This law restrained the soldier. He was being instructed that it is not acceptable to take such a woman and abuse her. The soldier who was attracted to this woman had to give her the full rights and status of marriage. She was to be treated as a fully-fledged wife. On no account could the soldier sexually use her because of his power and her vulnerability. Instead, she was to be brought into his home and given time to mourn:

> *The physical and emotional needs of the woman in her vulnerability are given moral and legal priority over the desires and claims of the man in his victorious strength.*[39]

---

38 Kathleen Nielson, *Women & God: Hard Questions, Beautiful Truth* (The Good Book Company, 2018), p. 66

39 Christopher Wright *New International Commentary: Deuteronomy* (Hendrickson Publishing,1996), pp. 234-235

The purpose of this law was to show that the woman must not be considered as property or spoils of war. Her personhood was not to be violated. If the soldier changed his mind and didn't want to fulfil his marital responsibility to her, she was not to be cast off. At the same time, she was not a prisoner and was free to leave if she wanted. You may wonder why God allowed the taking of women in war in any circumstance? We can speculate, but I believe the most likely explanation is that this brings a possible provision for her after her people have been defeated at Israel's hands and all seems lost. We are told of one woman who was brought into God's people after the defeat of her people in war. Her name was Rahab.[40] She sought refuge and received many blessings. Like Tamar before her, her son also became part of the ancestry of Jesus:

Abraham was the father of Isaac,
Isaac the father of Jacob,
Jacob the father of Judah and his brothers,
Judah the father of Perez and Zerah, whose mother was
Tamar,
Perez the father of Hezron,
Hezron the father of Ram,
Ram the father of Amminadab,
Amminadab the father of Nahshon,
Nahshon the father of Salmon,
Salmon the father of Boaz, whose mother was Rahab,
Boaz the father of Obed, whose mother was Ruth,

---

40 Joshua 2, 6:25

Obed the father of Jesse,
and Jesse the father of King David.[41]

Does God Treat Women Unjustly?

A man or woman who is a medium or spiritist among you must
be put to death. You are to stone them; their blood will be on
their own heads.[42]

The King James Bible, which was completed in 1611, translated this verse as:

A man also or woman that hath a familiar spirit, or that is a
wizard, shall surely be put to death: they shall stone them with
stones: their blood shall be upon them.

Stories about witches and wizards have been the backdrop to my children's childhood; we are *Harry Potter* and *Lord of the Rings* fans. I am not a supporter of the death penalty, and my perception of today's mediums is that they are mostly harmless charlatans. So I find these type of verses difficult. I am not alone. Elizabeth Cady Stanton hated this:

The actors in one of the blackest pages in human history,
claim Scriptural authority for their infernal deeds. Far
into the eighteenth century in England, the clergy dragged
innocent women into the courts as witches and learned judges
pronounced on them the sentence of torture and death. – While

---

41   Matthew 1:2-6

42   Leviticus 20:27

*women were tortured, drowned and burned by the thousands,
scarce one wizard to a hundred was ever condemned.*[43]

Lancaster, the city where I live, is famous for the 1612 Pendle witches trials. Out of the ten condemned, nine were women. Women were singled out. It is estimated that between the fifteenth and early eighteenth century in England there were around 500 executions of women for witchcraft. The figures for Europe as a whole are much higher, especially between 1580 and 1630 during the counter-reformation. The number is debated, but without a doubt, it is a shameful period. The Mosaic law was used to justify it. King James wrote a theological treatise in 1597 *Daemonologie* to outline the danger of witchcraft and encourage prosecution. The Bible handled poorly can explain whatever the reader wants it to and has been abused by powerful elites.

Nevertheless, some of these Old Testament laws can sound unnecessarily cruel and harsh. We must remember that these instructions were given to Israel as they sought to live as a holy nation in the ancient Middle East. These laws were given in a particular context. As Paul Copan explains:

Israel had bound herself to Yahweh, who had made a covenant with her ... The people had vowed that they were God's and that they would keep his covenant. They had willingly submitted to God's rule. So any intrusion into this relationship – whether in the form of foreign deities, political alliances or consulting with

---

43 Stanton, *The Woman's Bible*, p. iii

the dead – that replaced trust in God was in violation of these covenantal vows.[44]

The punishments may seem severe to us but as Copan goes on to say:

Of course, those not wanting to embrace Israel's God or obey his requirements were free to leave Israel and live in another nation. This was the obvious, preferable alternative.[45]

The law was a great equaliser. It did not single out women. Men and women were jointly capable and responsible for keeping God's covenant. However, there is one passage which describes the trial of a wife that does seem to single out women for different treatment:

Then the Lord said to Moses, 'Speak to the Israelites and say to them: "If a man's wife goes astray and is unfaithful to him so that another man has sexual relations with her, and this is hidden from her husband and her impurity is undetected (since there is no witness against her and she has not been caught in the act), and if feelings of jealousy come over her husband and he suspects his wife and she is impure – or if he is jealous and suspects her even though she is not impure – then he is to take his wife to the priest. He must also take an offering of a tenth of an ephah of barley flour on her behalf. He must not pour olive oil on it or put incense on it, because it is a grain offering for jealousy, a reminder-offering to draw attention to wrongdoing.

---

44   Copan, *Is God a Moral Monster?*, p. 92

45   ibid.

"'The priest shall bring her and make her stand before the Lord. Then he shall take some holy water in a clay jar and put some dust from the tabernacle floor into the water. After the priest has made the woman stand before the Lord, he shall loosen her hair and place in her hands the reminder-offering, the grain offering for jealousy, while he himself holds the bitter water that brings a curse. Then the priest shall put the woman under oath and say to her, 'If no other man has had sexual relations with you and you have not gone astray and become impure while married to your husband, may this bitter water that brings a curse not harm you. But if you have gone astray while married to your husband and you have made yourself impure by having sexual relations with a man other than your husband'– here the priest is to put the woman under this curse – 'may the Lord cause you to become a curse among your people when he makes your womb miscarry and your abdomen swell. May this water that brings a curse enter your body so that your abdomen swells or your womb miscarries.'

"'Then the woman is to say, 'Amen. So be it.'

"'The priest is to write these curses on a scroll and then wash them off into the bitter water. He shall make the woman drink the bitter water that brings a curse, and this water that brings a curse and causes bitter suffering will enter her. The priest is to take from her hands the grain offering for jealousy, wave it before the Lord and bring it to the altar. The priest is then to take a handful of the grain offering as a memorial offering and burn it on the altar; after that, he is to make the woman drink the water. If she has made herself impure and been unfaithful to her husband, this will be the result: when she is made to drink the water that brings a curse and causes bitter suffering, it will enter her, her abdomen will swell and her womb will miscarry, *and she will become a curse. If, however, the woman has not made herself impure, but is clean, she will be cleared of guilt and will be able to have children.*

"'This, then, is the law of jealousy when a woman goes astray and makes herself impure while married to her husband, or when feelings of jealousy come over a man because he suspects his wife. The priest is to make her stand before the Lord and is to apply this entire law to her. The husband will be innocent of any wrongdoing, but the woman will bear the consequences of her sin."[46]

This looks like a trial by ordeal. Ancient codes such as the Code of Hammurabi had life-threatening trials which required women to throw themselves into the river. Early modern history in Europe subjected women to similar fates. But this trial is not life-threatening. It is more along the lines of swearing an oath in court, although in this case, it involves drinking dusty water. As we reflect on this, we discover something unique.

This is the only Biblical law where the outcome depends upon a miracle – the whole case is taken out of human hands and placed before the Judge of the universe, who promises to judge righteously and render the verdict himself by supernatural means.[47]

The wife is protected from unfair accusation by a jealous husband. This trial is a means to protect her. She is innocent until proven guilty, unlike trials by ordeal.

---

46   Numbers 5:11-31

47   Davidson *Flame of Yahweh*, p. 352

Does God Consider Women Unclean?

The Lord said to Moses, 'Say to the Israelites: "A woman who becomes pregnant and gives birth to a son will be ceremonially unclean for seven days, just as she is unclean during her monthly period. On the eighth day the boy is to be circumcised. Then the woman must wait thirty-three days to be purified from her bleeding. She must not touch anything sacred or go to the sanctuary until the days of her purification are over. If she gives birth to a daughter, for two weeks the woman will be unclean, as during her period. Then she must wait sixty-six days to be purified from her bleeding.

"'When the days of her purification for a son or daughter are over, she is to bring to the priest at the entrance to the tent of meeting a year-old lamb for a burnt offering and a young pigeon or a dove for a sin offering. He shall offer them before the Lord to make atonement for her, and then she will be ceremonially clean from her flow of blood.

"'These are the regulations for the woman who gives birth to a boy or a girl. But if she cannot afford a lamb, she is to bring two doves or two young pigeons, one for a burnt offering and the other for a sin offering. In this way the priest will make atonement for her, and she will be clean."[48]

The cleanliness laws are strange and alien to us. Many things were unclean in the Israelite community; being clean/unclean was a normal part of life. This cleanliness was not to do with ordinary hygiene but referred to the preparation of people before they could participate in the ceremonial life

---

48   Leviticus 12:1-8

of the community. The difference between being clean and unclean provided a continual reminder that Israel needed to be prepared before they could approach God, who was holy and separate from them. This worship system was a visual illustration that humanity, in its natural fallen condition, cannot get close to God. It continues to show our need for God Himself to clean us to enable us to have a relationship with Him.

One area of ordinary life that came under these restrictions concerned women who were considered unclean during their regular monthly period. This is not a value judgement on women. They were not perceived as inherently more unclean than men; all discharges were regarded in the same way. Carol Meyers points out:

> These sex-related taboos are linked with other physical conditions, some linked to males and some sexually neutral.[49]

Sexual intercourse, a regular part of married life, made a couple 'unclean' – both men and women. To understand why sexual intercourse was viewed this way, we must remember that their ceremonial life was to be radically different from the pagan fertility practices of the nations around them. There was to be no confusion for Israel; sex and the sanctuary were to be separate. Worship in Israel was not about fertility practices. All the ordinary parts of family life that might be misused in the ceremonial life of Israel were subject to these restrictions.[50]

---

49   Davidson *Flame of Yahweh*, pp. 246-247

50   Leviticus 15

This, however, does not explain why a mother who gives birth to a girl appears to be more unclean than if she had given birth to a boy. What is going on here? All births in Israel were celebrated as a blessing. The cleansing process was part of the celebration for both boys and girls. The offerings were identical whatever the sex of the baby. A girl did not require a less valuable offering. In that way, boys and girls were equal. So what is going on?

Some have observed that vaginal bleeding can occur in newborn girls due to the withdrawal of the mother's oestrogen. They suggest the cleansing period was doubled to acknowledge both the mother and the daughter's flow of blood.[51] Other scholars suggest that separating mother and daughter from the tabernacle was to avoid the temptation to engage in the fertility practices of Near Eastern polytheism.[52] This would fit with the aims of the law. An alternative suggestion is that the period of uncleanness safeguarded a woman following childbirth. Having a longer recovery time following the birth of a daughter cushioned her from being made to try for a son too soon after delivery. Probably all of these things play a part.

Conclusion

I hope you can begin to see that the law, although culturally alien to us, is good. It established a means for Israel to worship God in a new and distinct way; a relationship in which women were included. It provided safety for women in the harsh ancient world. Finally, it is crucial to recognise that all of these

51 Davidson *Flame of Yahweh*, p. 246

52 Copan, *Is God a Moral Monster?*, p. 106

laws were temporary. The law was a shadow that pointed to eternal realities. It provided a social structure for Israel at the time while revealing humanity's need to be made pure before God. The sacrificial ceremonies were a kind of trailer that pointed to the real sacrifice that Jesus came to bring. The law continues to point to Jesus, although we no longer live under its regulations. It has been superseded by the new covenant He established. His work makes us permanently clean. His death on the cross changed everything:

> *The blood of goats and bulls and the ashes of a heifer sprinkled on those who are ceremonially unclean sanctify them so that they are outwardly clean. How much more, then, will the blood of Christ, who through the eternal Spirit offered himself unblemished to God, cleanse our consciences from acts that lead to death, so that we may serve the living God!*[53]

> *For by one sacrifice he has made perfect for ever those who are being made holy.*[54]

He opened up a new way for us to approach God without the complex system of sacrifices, temple worship, and priests. Jesus, and not those rituals, is what we need to have a relationship with God. Although the law remains to point to Jesus' work as our true priest and perfect sacrifice.

If you read the law in the context of the ancient world in which it was given, it stands as a miraculous document. The goodness of God in providing law that not only helped a sinful people live together as a nation, implementing justice, and

---

53   Hebrews 9:13-14

54   Hebrews 10:14

keeping order but also contained an extraordinary revelation. It displays our need for rescue while pointing to the means of that rescue: our Lord and Saviour Jesus Christ. We fear the law is all about restrictions on our behaviour; instead, it is truly life-giving. Well might the Psalmist say:

The law of the Lord is perfect,
refreshing the soul.
The statutes of the Lord are trustworthy,
making wise the simple.
The precepts of the Lord are right,
giving joy to the heart.
The commands of the Lord are radiant,
giving light to the eyes.
The fear of the Lord is pure,
enduring for ever.
The decrees of the Lord are firm,
and all of them are righteous.
They are more precious than gold,
than much pure gold;
they are sweeter than honey,
than honey from the honeycomb.[55]

FOR FURTHER THOUGHT AND CONVERSATION

- What would happen to a society that did not have any laws?
- How did Israel's law protect them?
- How do you feel about God's law?
- What does the law show us about what God is like?

55 Psalm 19:7-10

READ PSALM 119:1-16, 33-40

- How does the Psalmist feel about God's law?
- What is his desire?
- Why does he value God's words so much?
- Can you identify with the Psalmist?

9 WISDOM FOR ALL

Malala Yousafzai loved school, but everything changed when the Taliban took control of her town. Girls were forbidden to go to school, but she continued. Gunmen heard about her, sought her out and shot her in the left side of her head when she was travelling home on the school bus. Following a lengthy recovery, she continued in education and became the youngest-ever Nobel Laureate. She has established a charity, The Malala Fund, which seeks to champion every girl's right to twelve years of free, safe, quality education.[1] Threats to girls' education comes from various places. In some communities, it is sacrificed because it is considered unnecessary and too expensive. Elena Ferrante portrayed this conflict in her bestselling Neapolitan novels as a father and son discuss whether or not to send Lila to school. Both of them had learnt a trade instead of continuing with school, so the idea

---

1   https://www.malala.org/about Last accessed May 2021

that education was appropriate for a girl was inconceivable for Lila's father:

> *'Did you go to school?'*
> *'No.'*
> *'Then why should your sister, who is a girl, go to school?'*[2]

Marion Reid, who wrote one of the earliest feminist texts in 1843 challenged this expectation that a woman's sphere is domestic:

> *There are those who think that a woman's sphere really and truly comprises only her domestic duties, and that her mind ought never to stir beyond these.*[3]

The Bible does not teach that women are to be confined to domestic duties. If God considered it inappropriate for women to extend themselves beyond the home, and not engage in business, society, or culture, then one part of the Bible would not have been written! In Proverbs we have a portrait of a woman for everyone to learn from, and praise. It is magnificent! We meet her in this poem:

> *A wife of noble character who can find?*
> *She is worth far more than rubies.*
> *Her husband has full confidence in her*
> *and lacks nothing of value.*
> *She brings him good, not harm,*
> *all the days of her life.*
> *She selects wool and flax*

---

2   Elena Ferrante, *My Brilliant Friend* (Europa editions, 2012)

3   Marion Reid, *A Plea for Women* (1843), (Polygon, 1988), p. 8

and works with eager hands.
She is like the merchant ships,
bringing her food from afar.
She gets up while it is still night;
she provides food for her family
and portions for her female servants.
She considers a field and buys it;
out of her earnings she plants a vineyard.
She sets about her work vigorously;
her arms are strong for her tasks.
She sees that her trading is profitable,
and her lamp does not go out at night.
In her hand she holds the distaff
and grasps the spindle with her fingers.
She opens her arms to the poor
and extends her hands to the needy.
When it snows, she has no fear for her household;
for all of them are clothed in scarlet.
She makes coverings for her bed;
she is clothed in fine linen and purple.
Her husband is respected at the city gate,
where he takes his seat among the elders of the land.
She makes linen garments and sells them,
and supplies the merchants with sashes.
She is clothed with strength and dignity;
she can laugh at the days to come.
She speaks with wisdom,
and faithful instruction is on her tongue.
She watches over the affairs of her household
and does not eat the bread of idleness.
Her children arise and call her blessed;
her husband also, and he praises her:

'Many women do noble things,
  but you surpass them all.'
Charm is deceptive, and beauty is fleeting;
  but a woman who fears the Lord is to be praised.
Honour her for all that her hands have done,
  and let her works bring her praise at the city gate.[4]

The Bible is sometimes blamed for limiting women's lives yet this woman is so capable that the French philosopher and writer Simone de Beauvior complained:

Woman is doomed to immorality, because for her to be moral would mean that she must incarnate a being of superhuman qualities: the virtuous woman of Proverbs.[5]

Elisabeth Cady Stanton, however, praised this 'virtuous woman' suggesting that every woman should have her description framed and hung up in their homes.[6] I admit I find this woman intimidating, not least because she can work late at night and still get up early in the morning. She is a brilliant multi-tasker; housewife, and businesswoman. She can juggle everything, well might Simone de Beauvoir call her superhuman. I don't know anyone who completely fits her description. It's exhausting just thinking about doing what she manages to fit in. However, this description is encouraging. This housewife-come-businesswoman is a poetic construction. Each line of the poem starts with a consecutive letter of the Hebrew alphabet. It creates a figure we can visualise that is

---

4   Proverbs 31:10-31

5   De Beauvoir, *The Second Sex*, p. 492

6   Stanton, *The Woman's Bible*, p. 105.

not there to doom us to failure but to put flesh on the bones of teaching that has gone before. She is the embodiment of wisdom, demonstrating the essential quality of life:

'Many women do noble things,
    but you surpass them all.'
Charm is deceptive, and beauty is fleeting;
    but a woman who fears the Lord is to be praised.

The Proverbs woman surpasses everyone else not because she is so capable but because she fears the Lord. The things she does flow from that. Relating to God rightly matters above all else. The book of Proverbs calls us to this relationship. It leaves us in no doubt about what is needed to have a wise life:

The fear of the Lord is the beginning of wisdom, and knowledge of the Holy One is understanding.[7]

Acknowledging the Lord as opposed to the foolishness of ignoring Him underpins the book of Proverbs. With this in place, the text is full of observations and advice for wise living. It tackles a variety of subjects describing good behaviour and foolish behaviour. The book ends by drawing these threads together in an incredible portrayal of a woman. This depiction stands in stark contrast to cultures which have demeaned women and underestimated their potential. Ann Bradstreet, a committed Christian who became America's first published poet, battled with this in a poem written in 1643:

---

7   Proverbs 9:10

Let such as say our sex is void of reason,
Know 'tis a slander now, but once was treason.[8]

She objected to the idea that women were thought intellectually inferior to men and pointed to Elizabeth I to prove her case. Her poems are still in print, but at the time, there were many barriers to getting them into circulation. Her brother-in-law secretly took copies of her manuscripts from New England to London to find a publisher in 1650. In getting her work published, he had to make the following defence:

I doubt not but the reader will quickly find more than I can say [in these verses], and the worst effect of his reading will be unbelief, which will make him question whether it be a woman's work, and ask, is it possible? If any do, take this answer from him that dares avow it: it is the work of a woman, honoured and esteemed where she lives...[9]

In Christian communities such as the one that Ann Bradstreet was part of, women were 'honoured and esteemed'; although it would be several centuries before women were more widely published. However, Christian women did have the opportunity to engage in life beyond the domestic:

One of the remarkable features of post-Civil War America through the turn of the century was the vigorous activity of American evangelical women in social reform and missions.

8   Ann Bradstreet 'In Honor of that High and Mighty Princess Queen Elizabeth of Happy Memory,' https://www.poetryfoundation.org/poets/anne-bradstreet accessed July 2017

9   Faith Cook, *Anne Bradstreet: Pilgrim and Poet* (EP Books, 2010) p. 100

...The work of these women was so pioneering that numerous scholars have connected their activity to the beginnings of the secular feminist movement, including the suffrage movement.[10]

These Christian women were free to extend their sphere, particularly in charitable concerns because it was seen as appropriate Christian discipleship. Michelle Lee-Barnewall makes the case that it wasn't until World War 2 and the Cold War that women's lives in 1950s America were pushed back towards the domestic. Having a job outside of the home was seen as endangering the family:

In a period of uncertainty and transition, the home played a vital role in grounding Americans. In contrast to the more corporate concerns and assumptions at the turn of the century, Americans now began to turn inward to view their homes as their main source of identity and concern.[11]

It was 1950s America that caused Betty Friedan such problems. Betty Friedan gave voice to many when she said: 'I want something more than my husband and my children and home.' At that time, women were encouraged to be fulfilled as housewives and dare not dream of anything else. Sadly the church often backed this up. In an article that was entitled 'Jesus and the Liberated Woman', Billy Graham wrote this:

The biological assignment was basic and simple: Eve was to be the child-bearer, and Adam was to be the breadwinner ...

---

10   Michelle Lee-Barnewall, *Neither Complementarian nor Egalitarian* (Baker Academic, 2016), p. 19

11   ibid. p. 38

wife, mother, homemaker — this the appointed destiny of real womanhood.[12]

Some of these ideas spilt across the Atlantic to our shores too. Stereotypical images of Christian homemakers were encouraged. Don't get me wrong – for a woman to work at home is valuable. I spent many years doing it myself. C.S. Lewis once put it like this in a letter:

A housewife's work ...is surely, in reality, the most important work in the world. What do ships, railways, mines, cars, government, etc. exist for except that people may be fed, warmed, and safe in their own homes? As Dr. Johnson said, 'To be happy at home is the end of all human endeavour...so your job is one for which all others exist.'[13]

Homemaking is valuable, but the Bible does not insist on one particular sphere for women. We have already seen in Genesis that God does not limit women to the role of homemaker. There is freedom for women to express themselves in a wide variety of ways. Women can be engaged in every walk of life. However, the Bible was written in the ancient world when everyone's life was restricted. Men and women had tasks to perform, and choice did not come into it. If you were the son of a fisherman, you would become a fisherman. Women's lives were played out in the domestic arena. This did not mean that

---

12 Billy Graham 'Jesus and the Liberated Woman', Ladies Home journal, Dec (1970) p. 42.

13 A letter to Mrs Johnson March 16, 1955, http://www.essentialcslewis. com/2016/01/23/ccslq-19-homemakerultimate-career/ Last accessed May 2021

women were intellectually inferior to men. Indeed, in the Bible story, we meet some remarkable women who stand out because of their wisdom. Hannah is one such figure.

Hannah knew theological truths that others around her knew nothing about. She was looking forward to God's promised King and is the first person in the Bible to use the term 'the anointed one', which is more familiar to us as 'the Christ' or 'the Messiah'. She lived during the period of the Judges. It was a time of terrible corruption. The Word of the Lord was rarely heard, but Hannah knew what God was like. She poured out her heart to God in her pain and praised Him in her joy. Her prophetic prayer reveals her deep knowledge of God:

My heart rejoices in the Lord;
  in the Lord my horn is lifted high.
My mouth boasts over my enemies,
  for I delight in your deliverance.

There is no one holy like the Lord;
  there is no one besides you;
  there is no Rock like our God.

Do not keep talking so proudly
  or let your mouth speak such arrogance,
for the Lord is a God who knows,
  and by him deeds are weighed.

The bows of the warriors are broken,
  but those who stumbled are armed with strength.
Those who were full hire themselves out for food,

but those who were hungry are hungry no more.
She who was barren has borne seven children,
  but she who has had many sons pines away.

The Lord brings death and makes alive;
  he brings down to the grave and raises up.
The Lord sends poverty and wealth;
  he humbles and he exalts.
He raises the poor from the dust
  and lifts the needy from the ash heap;
he seats them with princes
  and makes them inherit a throne of honour.

For the foundations of the earth are the Lord's;
  on them he has set the world.
He will guard the feet of his faithful servants,
  but the wicked will be silenced in the place of darkness.

It is not by strength that one prevails;
  those who oppose the Lord will be broken.
The Most High will thunder from heaven;
  the Lord will judge the ends of the earth.

He will give strength to his king
  and exalt the horn of his anointed.[14]

Hannah may have lived in a domestic sphere, but she had a wisdom that sustained her. This unlikely woman was used by God to proclaim prophetic truths. She knew God was capable of turning the understanding of the world upside down. She

---

14 1 Samuel 2:1-10

understood that it was not going to be through the strength of a warrior that God would bring about His kingdom. Her words look forward to Jesus, who brought victory, not in battle but weakness, when He was led like a lamb to slaughter.

If Hannah surprises us, it is because we have misunderstood God. He doesn't think women are devoid of reason. He doesn't tell women not to bother their pretty little heads with deep things. God chose Hannah to teach her nation about the coming Christ. She was an unlikely candidate. Her life wasn't always easy, but her constant dependence on God led to wisdom that still speaks to us.

Another such woman was Abigail. Let's look at her story in full. Unusually she is described as intelligent. Only one other person in the Bible is commented on in this way. Abigail, being married to a wealthy landowner, had responsibility and authority over her large household, managing servants. Her husband, Nabal, was known to be a 'fool' so you can imagine that she spent a lot of time resolving the problems that he had caused. One episode triggered a crisis that nearly destroyed her household:

While David was in the wilderness, he heard that Nabal was shearing sheep. So he sent ten young men and said to them, 'Go up to Nabal at Carmel and greet him in my name. Say to him: "Long life to you! Good health to you and your household! And good health to all that is yours!

"'Now I hear that it is sheep-shearing time. When your shepherds were with us, we did not ill-treat them, and the whole time they were at Carmel nothing of theirs was missing.

Ask your own servants and they will tell you. Therefore be favourable towards my men, since we come at a festive time. Please give your servants and your son David whatever you can find for them."'

When David's men arrived, they gave Nabal this message in David's name. Then they waited.

Nabal answered David's servants, 'Who is this David? Who is this son of Jesse? Many servants are breaking away from their masters these days. Why should I take my bread and water, and the meat I have slaughtered for my shearers, and give it to men coming from who knows where?'

David's men turned round and went back. When they arrived, they reported every word. David said to his men, 'Each of you strap on your sword!' So they did, and David strapped his on as well. About four hundred men went up with David, while two hundred stayed with the supplies.

One of the servants told Abigail, Nabal's wife, 'David sent messengers from the wilderness to give our master his greetings, but he hurled insults at them. Yet these men were very good to us. They did not ill-treat us, and the whole time we were out in the fields near them nothing was missing. Night and day they were a wall around us the whole time we were herding our sheep near them. Now think it over and see what you can do, because disaster is hanging over our master and his whole household. He is such a wicked man that no one can talk to him.'[15]

---

15   1 Samuel 25:4-17

Abigail's servants knew she would know what to do in this life-threatening situation. They were right. Facing this potential catastrophe, Abigail acted immediately:

Abigail acted quickly. She took two hundred loaves of bread, two skins of wine, five dressed sheep, five seahs of roasted grain, a hundred cakes of raisins and two hundred cakes of pressed figs, and loaded them on donkeys. Then she told her servants, 'Go on ahead; I'll follow you.' But she did not tell her husband Nabal.

As she came riding her donkey into a mountain ravine, there were David and his men descending towards her, and she met them. David had just said, 'It's been useless – all my watching over this fellow's property in the wilderness so that nothing of his was missing. He has paid me back evil for good. May God deal with David, be it ever so severely, if by morning I leave alive one male of all who belong to him!'

When Abigail saw David, she quickly got off her donkey and bowed down before David with her face to the ground. She fell at his feet and said: 'Pardon your servant, my lord, and let me speak to you; hear what your servant has to say. Please pay no attention, my lord, to that wicked man Nabal. He is just like his name – his name means Fool, and folly goes with him. And as for me, your servant, I did not see the men my lord sent. And now, my lord, as surely as the Lord your God lives and as you live, since the Lord has kept you from bloodshed and from avenging yourself with your own hands, may your enemies and all who are intent on harming my lord be like Nabal. And let this gift, which your servant has brought to my lord, be given to the men who follow you.

'Please forgive your servant's presumption. The Lord your God will certainly make a lasting dynasty for my lord, because you fight the Lord's battles, and no wrongdoing will be found in you as long as you live. Even though someone is pursuing you to take your life, the life of my lord will be bound securely in the bundle of the living by the Lord your God, but the lives of your enemies he will hurl away as from the pocket of a sling. When the Lord has fulfilled for my lord every good thing he promised concerning him and has appointed him ruler over Israel, my lord will not have on his conscience the staggering burden of needless bloodshed or of having avenged himself. And when the Lord your God has brought my lord success, remember your servant.'

David said to Abigail, 'Praise be to the Lord, the God of Israel, who has sent you today to meet me. May you be blessed for your good judgment and for keeping me from bloodshed this day and from avenging myself with my own hands. Otherwise, as surely as the Lord, the God of Israel, lives, who has kept me from harming you, if you had not come quickly to meet me, not one male belonging to Nabal would have been left alive by daybreak.'

Then David accepted from her hand what she had brought to him and said, 'Go home in peace. I have heard your words and granted your request.'[16]

The threat of violence from David must have been daunting. David was not known for losing battles. However, Abigail was a superb mediator. Her plea for mercy revealed that she knew the promises of God and understood their implications.

---

16   1 Samuel 25:18-35

Controversially, albeit very gently, she dared to challenge David, the king in waiting. Abigail became David's prophet and teacher; she was brave enough to speak truth to power. By doing so, she prevented God's chosen king from committing a horrible act of bloodshed. Her intervention protected David from becoming as murderous as the failed king he would replace. When David realised this, he praised God for sending her. Abigail had saved him from perpetrating a brutal act of vengeance. She not only protected her household but the integrity of David's future kingship. His kingship mattered because he was a forerunner of that greater King, Jesus, who came to rescue the world and not condemn it. God's King is just. He must be seen to be just.

Hannah and Abigail are woven into Israel's story, although their lives appear to be played out in the domestic sphere. Hannah was a mother, and Abigail, a problem-solving wife. They had very different experiences: Hannah wept many tears; Abigail had many responsibilities. However, both feared the Lord above all else and sought refuge in Him. Consequentially God used them to reveal profound theological truths. These women ended up speaking way beyond the domestic sphere. How does God feel about women? Despite our fears that women do not feature in the Bible story, we see that they are given a prophetic voice which points to Jesus.

It must grieve God's heart when women are devalued, refused education, and held back from all that they could be. There is nothing in the Bible that supports this. Conversely, women are encouraged to take hold of knowledge and apply it. There is considerable freedom for women to engage in intellectual pursuits, choose challenging careers, or work at home or in their communities. But their minds should stir beyond the domestic sphere, and their eyes should be raised far beyond career opportunities. God's Word encourages women to lift their thoughts to even higher things and to seek true wisdom. The wisdom that begins by fearing Him. This wisdom is hard to find:

> *Where then does wisdom come from?*
> *Where does understanding dwell?*
> *It is hidden from the eyes of every living thing,*
> *concealed even from the birds in the sky.*
> *Destruction and Death say,*
> *'Only a rumour of it has reached our ears.'*
> *God understands the way to it*
> *and he alone knows where it dwells,*
> *for he views the ends of the earth*
> *and sees everything under the heavens.*[17]

But this wisdom can be found no matter what life circumstances you face. It is available for everyone. God has not excluded women from it; Hannah and Abigail show us that. It is a gift from God, and we only need to seek it:

> *Indeed, if you call out for insight*
> *and cry aloud for understanding,*
> *and if you look for it as for silver*
> *and search for it as for hidden treasure,*
> *then you will understand the fear of the Lord*
> *and find the knowledge of God.*

---

17   Job 28:20-24

For the Lord gives wisdom;
   from his mouth come knowledge and understanding.[18]

FOR FURTHER THOUGHT AND CONVERSATION

- What do you think makes a person wise?
- Are you surprised by the description of the 'wife of noble character'?
- Which of her qualities stand out for you?
- What do you think it means to 'fear the Lord'?

READ 1 CORINTHIANS 1:18-30

- What do you think about the way the Bible understands wisdom?
- What would it look like for you to seek wisdom?

---

18   Proverbs 2:3-6

10 THE BROKEN BRIDE

When the media criticised Taylor Swift for her relationships, she penned a song. She compared herself to Leonardo DeCaprio, well known for having many girlfriends, and imagined how she would be perceived if she were a man:

I would be complex, I would be cool
They'd say I played the field before I found someone to commit
to
And that would be okay for me to do
Every conquest I had made would make me more of a boss to
you ...
I'd be just like Leo in Saint-Tropez
... I'd be the man[1]

The Twitter response to Taylor's song was enthusiastic. Lots of voices declared with her: 'if I were a man, I'd be the man'. One tweet, however, read: 'You don't need to be The Man because you're THE WOMAN and that is so much more powerful.'

---

1   Taylor Swift, 'The Man', from the 2019 album, *Lover*

There is a long history of inconsistency and double standards regarding women's sexuality. Women are not supposed to make conquests. Yet this terrain is increasingly complex. Naomi Wolf argued that since the sexual revolution of the 1960s virginity is mocked, but sexual liberation has come at a price:

Virgin? What's your problem? Whore? What's your number?[2]

The sexual liberation movement brought with it pressure for women to be more sexually active, which in turn has left them vulnerable to abuse. In recent years the dark side of this sexual liberation has become increasingly evident. The #MeToo movement has revealed the use of intimidation and power behind some of this so-called sexual freedom. There are various campaigns across the world, such as: 'Say No!' or 'Not on' to sexual coercion and harassment. At last, some change is happening. Attitudes that were previously deemed to be acceptable are viewed with new eyes. For instance, watching the original *Bladerunner* movie from 1982, the 'romantic' scene between the two central characters is uncomfortable. The scene is now discussed in fan forums as coercion and possibly rape.

Predatory sexual behaviour by men is condemned today, although as Taylor Swift observed, society still grants men licence to be promiscuous, but not women. Some women are embracing a new sexual freedom, as seen in Cardi B's

---

2   Naomi Wolf, Promiscuities: *The Secret History of Female Desire* (London: Vintage, 1998), p. 131

controversial hit single 'WAP'.[3] Navigating this landscape is challenging. The rules have changed and yet remain. Which persona should someone adopt, the Madonna or the Whore? Are there only two choices? Is it liberating to declare: 'I'll be the man'? What does it mean to be 'the Woman'? What are the rules? How should we conduct ourselves well as sexual people? Does the Bible view women as either virginal or deviant? Simone de Beauvoir in *The Second Sex* blamed Christianity for trapping women in an impossible ideal in which their sexuality was seen as both simultaneously abhorrent and necessary.[4] How does the Bible view the sexuality of women? Let's take each image in turn.

The Madonna

Is it true that the Bible traps women in the impossible problem of being virginal and yet mothers? The image of the Madonna comes from Catholicism; Mary, the mother of Jesus, has been venerated as a saint who was perpetually a virgin, free of sin, mother of God, and able to intercede on our behalf. Beauvoir rightly says this is unattainable. But this view of Mary does not come from the gospel witnesses. This is a fiction that developed outside of Scripture. Look at just a few of the things this mythology ignores:

---

3 https://www.telegraph.co.uk/music/what-to-listen-to/pornography-feminist-triumph-cardi-bs-wap-video-started-culture/ accessed October 2020

4 De Beauvoir, *The Second Sex*, p. 203

MARY WAS NOT ALWAYS A VIRGIN

She conceived of the Holy Spirit as a virgin, and when she gave birth to Jesus, she was a virgin. However, she went on to have a regular marital life. She slept with her husband:

> When Joseph woke up, he did what the angel of the Lord had commanded him and took Mary home as his wife. But he did not consummate their marriage until she gave birth to a son. And he gave him the name Jesus.[5]

She had other children after Jesus: 'Then Jesus' mother and brothers arrived. Standing outside, they sent someone in to call him.'[6]

MARY WAS NOT PERFECT

At the beginning of His ministry, Mary failed to understand who Jesus was or what He had come to do. She got things wrong. At one point, she and her other sons even tried to stop Jesus from teaching:

> When his family heard about this, they went to take charge of him, for they said, 'He is out of his mind...' Then Jesus' mother and brothers arrived. Standing outside, they sent someone in to call him. A crowd was sitting around him, and they told him, 'Your mother and brothers are outside looking for you.' 'Who are my mother and my brothers?' he asked. Then he looked at those seated in a circle around him and said, 'Here

---

5   Matthew 1:24-25

6   Mark 3:31

are my mother and my brothers! Whoever does God's will is my brother and sister and mother.[7]

Mary was an ordinary woman who was given an extraordinary responsibility.

Mary knew that in becoming the mother to Jesus, she was given a privilege that she did not deserve. She did not exalt herself, but God:

And Mary said: 'My soul glorifies the Lord and my spirit rejoices in God my Saviour, for he has been mindful of the humble state of his servant. From now on all generations will call me blessed, for the Mighty One has done great things for me— holy is his name.'[8]

MARY KNEW GOD AS HER SAVIOUR

Mary made no claims for herself. She was the descendant of Eve who gave birth to the long-promised serpent crusher. She was honoured to become the mother of Jesus, although that came with a cost. She had to learn who Jesus was and to submit to His wisdom. A sword pierced her heart when He was nailed to the cross, and she watched Him die in agony. But she was there to experience the joy of His resurrection. She was part of the group in Jerusalem, along with her sons, who gathered together and prayed as they waited for the promised Holy Spirit. She saw it all: Jesus' birth, His ministry, His death, His resurrection, His ascension, and the beginning of the church on the day of Pentecost. What happened next

7   Mark 3:21, 31-35

8   Luke 1:46-49

in her life the Bible accounts do not say. The part she played was incredible, but it was always about Jesus. Jesus is the only sinless person who has lived. Jesus is the only rescuer. Jesus is the one who continues to intercede for us as He sits at His Father's right hand in heaven. Jesus is the one we are called to follow, not an impossible ideal of womanhood.

The Whore

The Bible does contain depictions of prostitution and adultery, particularly in the books of the prophets. The language used is graphic:

> *As soon as she saw them, she lusted after them and sent messengers to them in Chaldea. Then the Babylonians came to her, to the bed of love, and in their lust they defiled her. After she had been defiled by them, she turned away from them in disgust …she became more and more promiscuous as she recalled the days of her youth, when she was a prostitute in Egypt. There she lusted after her lovers, whose genitals were like those of donkeys and whose emission was like that of horses. So you longed for the lewdness of your youth, when in Egypt your bosom was caressed and your young breasts fondled.*[9]

This picture of lustful unfaithfulness recurs over and over again, but it's not describing a particular woman; instead, it is a metaphor illustrating the faithlessness of the people of Israel. Through this imagery, the prophets expressed the brokenness of the people's relationship with God. When Israel kept on turning to other gods and ignoring God, they were like a

---

9   Ezekiel 23:16-21

wife rejecting her husband and desiring other lovers. The earthy language conveys the pain and horror of spiritual unfaithfulness.

But why does the Bible use women's unfaithfulness as the metaphor of choice? Why not the adulterous husband? It feels unfair – after all the adulterous and unfaithful husband is (dare I say this) more common than that of the wife. In the 2016 film adaptation of Jane Austen's *Lady Susan, Love and friendship*, Sir James Martin makes this comment:

> *For a husband to wander is not the same as vice versa – if a husband strays he is merely responding to his biology – it is how men are made but for a woman to act in a similar way is ridiculous, unimaginable, just the idea is funny.*[10]

This is the double standard Taylor Swift sang about. So, does the Bible use the image of the unfaithful wife because female promiscuity is unnatural whereas the husband is free to stray? Is it used because women's unfaithfulness is far worse than that of men? Is it used because unconsciously the prophets had a negative view of women's sexuality? Is it as Simone de Beauvoir suggests that ultimately, women carry the weight of fallenness? When we dig into this, we discover the reason for this imagery is much more profound and extraordinarily beautiful. We find it when we read the prophet Hosea.

Hosea begins with an unconventional marriage. It turns out like a soap opera: boy marries girl, the girl is unfaithful, they have children, but he is not the father, she has many

---

10   *Love and Friendship*, dir. Whit Stillman, Amazon Studios Roadside Attraction, 2016

lovers, she leaves him and ends up in sexual slavery, a victim of grooming; the boy finds her, he pays for her freedom, brings her home and their marriage is restored. But this retelling of the story misses out a crucial detail from the plot: Hosea had been told by God to marry the kind of woman who would leave him:

> *When the Lord began to speak through Hosea, the Lord said to him, 'Go, marry a promiscuous woman and have children with her, for like an adulterous wife this land is guilty of unfaithfulness to the Lord.'[11]*

When Hosea announced he wanted to marry Gomer, I doubt his family celebrated, and I am sure his friends advised him against it. But he deliberately began a relationship with Gomer, a woman who would neglect him, deride him, leave him and then forget him. She was an impossible bride. His marriage brought him heartbreak and betrayal. However, God wanted to use Hosea's experience to help Israel understand that this is what their relationship with God was like. Did you notice how her adultery is described as a reflection of Israel's infidelity? As we follow this story, we learn that this unfaithfulness not only describes Israel, but it reflects the way that people from the beginning have cast God aside:

> *But like Adam they transgressed the covenant;*
> *there they dealt faithlessly with me.[12]*

---

11   Hosea 1:2

12   Hosea 6:7 (ESV) The Hebrew is unusual – the NIV chooses to translate it: 'As at Adam', with a footnote 'like human beings'.

Israel's sin is like Adam's sin, which reminds us of Eden and the first rejection of God. In Hosea's marriage to Gomer, we see our rejection of God played out. God used Hosea's marriage to help us understand the reality of our sin, of our hearts and our relationship with God.

At his wedding, Hosea knew he would be betrayed. When God rescued Israel, He knew Israel would betray Him. When God made the world, He knew we would turn from Him. God knows that by nature, we are the promiscuous wife: unfaithful, fickle, arrogant, and proud. He knows we seek satisfaction anywhere other than with Him, and we end up messed up. We are the impossible bride who rejects her husband and destroys herself in the process.

In stories when the girl betrays the boy, there are few happy endings. Othello murders his wife on the mere whisper of adultery. However, the story of Hosea and Gomer plays out very differently. God is the wronged husband who cries out to His faithless wife. It is a heartbroken love which is not reciprocated:

> *'What can I do with you, Ephraim?*
> *What can I do with you, Judah?*
> *Your love is like the morning mist,*
> *like the early dew that disappears.*[13]

Yet despite the heartache of this broken relationship, it is a love that does not give up:

---

13   Hosea 6:4

How can I give you up, Ephraim?
How can I hand you over, Israel?[14]

So God rescues His faithless bride by taking her into the wilderness to woo her.

Therefore I am now going to allure her;
I will lead her into the wilderness
and speak tenderly to her.[15]

This is beautiful. God gently attends to His broken people with much more than tender words. He takes His bride to the wilderness to restore her:

There I will give her back her vineyards,
and will make the Valley of Achor a door of hope.
There she will respond as in the days of her youth,
as in the day she came up out of Egypt.[16]

God rescues these troubled people, this broken bride. 'The Valley of Achor' means the Valley of Trouble. It was a notorious place associated with execution. It was the place where Achan had been punished because of his rebellion; it was a place of condemnation. But now it was to be a place of hope. Not only was God promising to call His faithless people back to Him, but He was declaring that He would remove the punishment they deserved!

Hosea preached this message of hope to the people of his day and publicly demonstrated it by reconciling with his wife.

---

14   Hosea 11:8

15   Hosea 2:14

16   Hosea 2:15

We have an even greater display of God's love for us. We see God's love in Christ's death on the cross. Jesus gave Himself up for us to bring us out of the wilderness and transform the Valley of Achor into a door of hope:

> *You see, at just the right time, when we were still powerless, Christ died for the ungodly. Very rarely will anyone die for a righteous person, though for a good person someone might possibly dare to die. But God demonstrates his own love for us in this: while we were still sinners, Christ died for us.*[17]

Christ took God's punishment for us!

> *For Christ also suffered once for sins, the righteous for the unrighteous, to bring you to God.*[18]

Jesus suffered for us knowing we were just like the Israelites, just like Gomer. We deserve wrath and trouble but instead are offered tender mercy. God transforms unruly people and rescues them in a way Hosea never fully understood because he lived many hundreds of years before Jesus.

Women's sexuality in the Bible is not singled out as decadent and transgressive. The imagery of the adulterous woman in the Old Testament is not there to diminish women but to graphically illustrate the brokenness of our relationship with God. The sexual intimacy between husband and wife is one of the closest bonds that we can know. It is for this reason that sexual unfaithfulness is used as a metaphor. It is there to help us grasp the impact of our rejection of God

---

17   Romans 5:6-8

18   1 Peter 3:18

and to feel the weight of our indifference and dismissal of God. Astonishingly, God does not give up on us, but instead, sacrificially saves us. This sexual imagery reveals the profound love of God. There is no suggestion that women are worse than men.

The Bible's message is clear; men and women need this rescue; we are all broken. No one has everything sorted, not one of us is perfect, and as a consequence, our sexuality is broken too. We see evidence of that all around us. On her album *Lover* Taylor Swift sings of this brokenness:

> *I've been the archer,*
> *I've been the prey*
> *Screaming, who could ever leave me, darling?*
> *But who could stay?*
> *I see right through me,*
> *'Cause they see right through me*
> *Can you see right through me?*
> *They see right through*
> *They see right through me*
> *I see right through me*
> *All the king's horses, all the king's men*
> *Couldn't put me together again*
> *'Cause all of my enemies started out friends*
> *Help me hold onto you.* [19]

Taylor describes her battle with self-love and low esteem. It's an honest song that lays bare emotions we all experience. Sometimes we allow ourselves to face these feelings head on and we can be overwhelmed by our brokenness and fearful

---

19   Taylor Swift, 'The Archer', from the 2019 album, *Lover*

that we can never be put back together again. We see right through ourselves and cannot imagine how anyone could ever love us. Taylor's song is a cry of desperation: who could ever love her? Who could ever love us? Can a perfect God who sees right through us love us? He promises to.

> *I will heal their waywardness*
>   *and love them freely,*
>   *for my anger has turned away from them.*[20]

God loves the unlovely. God loves the undeserving. We need not be afraid. He can sort us out.

For Further Thought and Conversation

- Do you think women's sexuality is viewed more negatively than men's in today's culture?
- Why do you think we experience so much brokenness in our sexual relationships?
- How do you expect someone to behave who has been betrayed by their partner?
- What do you think about God being described as the wronged husband?

Read Hosea 14:1-9

- What do God's people need to do?
- What is God's promise to them?
- Do you think you have turned away from God?
- What would it look like for you to return to God?

---

20   Hosea 14:4

11. THE WIFE

Some Christians give the impression that marriage is the ultimate goal in life. Women, in particular, are alienated by this if they have been taught that God's primary desire for them is to become wives and mothers. In these churches, marriage is presented as the means for a fulfilling life. Yet in reality, marriage has a chequered history. It is a flawed institution which has at times sanctioned physical, emotional and sexual abuse. In Elena Ferrante's Neapolitan novels set in the 1960s, Lila, imprisoned in a violent marriage, believed this:

> *We had grown up thinking that a stranger must not even touch us, but that our father, our boyfriend, and our husband could hit us when they liked, out of love, to educate us, to reeducate us.*[1]

This abuse is not fictional. Simone de Beauvoir hated the institution of marriage seeing tyranny as its inevitable fruit:

---

1   Elena Ferrante, *The Story of a New Name* (Europa Editions, 2013)

In marrying, the woman gets some share in the world as her own; legal guarantees protect her against capricious action by man; but she becomes his vassal.[2]

De Beauvoir, herself, chose to conduct a life-long 'open' marriage with Jean-Paul Sartre. Her philosophy was to be a significant catalyst for the second wave of feminism in the 1970s.

Women's lives have changed dramatically in the last fifty years, and many of the things that early second-wave feminists fought for have been won. Married women pursue various careers and maintain their economic independence. Marriage has been modernised. It is no longer true that:

marriage is the destiny offered to women by society...most women are married, or have been, or plan to be, or suffer from not being.[3]

The status of singleness has changed too. It no longer implies celibacy or childlessness, and choosing to be childfree is also a desirable option.

Christians' admiration of marriage is out of step with our culture, which raises lots of questions for us to consider. Does marriage matter anymore? What value does God place on marriage? Is marriage God's plan for men and women? Does marriage put women in a subordinate relationship? Does the Bible teach that singleness is second-best? Let's start with singleness.

---

2   De Beauvoir , *The Second Sex*, p. 449

3   ibid. p. 445

Singleness

In the past, an unmarried woman's options were severely limited. Hamlet told Ophelia: 'Get thee to a nunnery!' and he wasn't joking. Without the prospect of marriage, the convent was the only alternative sanctuary to family. In *Pride and Prejudice,* Jane Austen described the economic necessity of marriage for status and security; thus, Caroline Lucas married the odious Mr Collins:

> *I ask only a comfortable home; and considering Mr Collin's character, connections, and situation in life, I am convinced my chance of happiness with him is as fair as most people can boast on entering the marriage state.*[4]

The Brontë sisters wrote about the hardships of not being married and being forced to become governesses. This was one of the few opportunities for employment open to the middle-class woman in the nineteenth century. Twentieth-century women had limited choices too. As a child, I knew many older women who had lost their fiancés in the Great War. These women treasured the photos of the men they had loved. Spinsterhood was a word they carried into old age, mourning a life they never had. The workplace had been hostile, and only a few careers opened up to them. They became teachers, nurses and secretaries in a society that did not have equal opportunities or equal pay. They were legally unable to have a mortgage unless they had a male guarantor. Singleness had been difficult.

---

4   Jane Austen, *Pride and Prejudice* (1813), (Oxford University Press, 2004), p. 96

The Bible covers a timeframe of several thousand years from early tribal and kinship culture to Israel's nationhood and monarchy and finally to the Roman Empire. Each culture had different ways of managing family life, but marriage was constant:

a man leaves his father and mother and is united to his wife, and they become one flesh.[5]

People rarely chose singleness, although a few like Jeremiah were called to it:

Then the word of the Lord came to me: 'You must not marry and have sons or daughters in this place.'[6]

Celibacy was unusual; it was not demanded of priests nor prophets; on the contrary, marriage was the norm.

However, in the New Testament Paul taught that singleness was a good choice, a positive thing that could enable people, both men and women, to be free of family responsibilities and to give themselves wholeheartedly to the Lord's affairs.[7] The apostle Paul was single himself and considered it a great blessing:

I wish that all of you were as I am. But each of you has your own gift from God; one has this gift, another has that.[8]

---

5   Genesis 2:24

6   Jeremiah 16:1-2

7   1 Corinthians 7:32-35

8   1 Corinthians 7:7

Interestingly, he did not discriminate between men and women in this; he believed singleness was an excellent option for everyone. This is unusual. Traditionally societies have had less problem with single men, but single women have been stigmatised because there was no clear role for them outside of the family home. Paul, however, taught that both men and women could serve the Lord wholeheartedly outside of the institution of marriage. He envisioned a space for women to be engaged in meaningful activity that was other than wife and mother, and he believed that it was good if not better. This is not how we commonly think of women's roles in the Bible or the attitude we associate with Paul. It seems he was a man ahead of his time after all!

History records the lives of some single women who worked tirelessly for the cause of the gospel and social reform outside of the home. Florence Nightingale is a household name, but there were others, such as the missionary to Nigeria, Mary Slessor. She left her work in the Scottish mills to proclaim the gospel, but found herself intervening to stop the practice of killing twins, and trial by poison. She eventually became a local vice-consul and was asked by the local tribe to preside over the native court.[9] She was honoured in Nigeria. The lives of such women are often derided today for imposing their European values and colonialist attitudes on other cultures. They did not get everything right, their work had flaws but they did not get it all wrong; they achieved much. These women gave their lives to service. They knew with confident

---

9   W.P. Livingstone, *Mary Slessor of Calabar* (1927), (Lulu.com, 2018)

certainty that they had a task, a purpose, a calling that did not depend on marriage. They were bold and pioneering for the sake of others because they had a far higher calling. They were answering the call of Christ:

> *Then Jesus came to them and said, 'All authority in heaven and on earth has been given to me. Therefore go and make disciples of all nations, baptising them in the name of the Father and of the Son and of the Holy Spirit, and teaching them to obey everything I have commanded you. And surely I am with you always, to the very end of the age.'* [10]

Marriage

The teachings of Paul are often viewed with suspicion. He has been accused of being both sexist and a misogynist. After all, isn't it he who teaches that wives should obey their husbands? Hasn't his teaching led to the legitimisation of physical and emotional abuse in marriage? Isn't it him that spawned abuse such as that experienced by Ruth Tucker?

> *During his violent rages, my ex-husband often hurled Biblical texts at me, as though the principal tenet of Scripture was, 'Wives, submit to your husbands.' He'd spit the words out, repeatedly beating me over the head, at least figuratively, with his black-and-white Bible. His hitting and punching and slamming me against doors and furniture, however, were anything but figurative. Nor were his terror-loaded threats. I felt trapped and feared for my life ...* [11]

10   Matthew 28:18-20

11   Ruth Tucker, *Black and White Bible, Black and Blue Wife* (Zondervan, 2016)

This is appalling. You cannot overstate the horror of abuse such as this. The wife suffers not only the physical assault but the spiritual damage that is inevitable with the warping of the Bible's teaching. How hard for women who have experienced this ever to trust the Bible again. How difficult for them to hold on to the truth that God is good when His name is used to terrorise them. Abusers, at this level, believe that there is a natural order of male authority and female subordination, which is their right to enforce. This is horrendous, and I have never heard any pastor or minister advocate it. But abusive individuals have long hidden within the church and used the Bible as a licence. This is changing. Awareness of this danger is growing. Church leaders are beginning to be proactive in safeguarding and calling out misogynistic abuse for what it is. God disapproves of violence against women. We must understand what Paul taught about marriage correctly. Let's take a closer look:

Submit to one another out of reverence for Christ. Wives, submit yourselves to your own husbands as you do to the Lord. For the husband is the head of the wife as Christ is the head of the church, his body, of which he is the Saviour. Now as the church submits to Christ, so also wives should submit to their husbands in everything.

Husbands, love your wives, just as Christ loved the church and gave himself up for her to make her holy, cleansing her by the washing with water through the word, and to present her to himself as a radiant church, without stain or wrinkle or any other blemish, but holy and blameless. In this same way, husbands ought to love their wives as their own bodies. He who loves his wife loves himself. After all, no one ever hated their own body, but they feed and care for their body, just as Christ does the church – for we are members of his body. 'For this reason a man will leave his father and mother and be united to his wife, and the two will become one flesh.' This is a profound mystery – but I am talking about Christ and the church. However, each one of you also must love his wife as he loves himself, and the wife must respect her husband.[12]

I have seen two extreme responses to this passage: one is horror because it seems to advocate abuse; the other is easy acceptance because it fits the individual's stereotypes about male and female roles. Neither are right. The first thing to note is that Paul teaches that there is a difference between men and women regarding their responsibilities in marriage. It is this difference which has been used as a mandate by some for male dominance in marriage. A culture that believes men are superior to women has no difficulty taking this teaching to imply that men are to rule, and women are to obey. But what did Paul mean when he talked about wives submitting to their husbands? Is it that men are naturally in charge and should be served? To understand what Paul is teaching, we must read him carefully.

THE WIFE

The wife is called to submit as the church does to Christ. John Woodhouse described it like this:

---

12 Ephesians 5:21-33

The biblical teaching about wives submitting to their husbands is not ever about wives submitting to, accepting from or supporting evil actions or words from their husbands. To suggest otherwise is to turn the biblical teaching on its head. The bible calls on wives to submit to the love of their husbands – like submitting to Jesus, who died on the cross for us.[13]

The church submits to Christ joyfully; it is a voluntary response to the loving sacrifice of Jesus. This is the wife's calling. It is a joyful willingness to give herself to her husband. The way the Greek word for 'submit' is written reinforces this because grammatically it is something one does to oneself. Sarah Sumner expressed it like this:

The submission of a wife must be motivated by the personal will of the wife. In other words, the locus of control belongs to her. In that sense, he (the husband) does not lead her. She leads herself into submission. She voluntarily yields herself to him... Submission is a relational posture. It means 'coming under' her husband in order to lift him up in everything.[14]

This is not easy, yet if you have ever been in love or cared about someone deeply you will know the desire to submit to them, to value their ideas, to care about their happiness, to want to exalt them. It is to be profoundly other-person-centred. It is a posture of deep love. It is yielding oneself entirely to another. It is difficult, not because of our fears

13   John Woodhouse, 'Abigail: A godly woman with a fool for a husband? (1 Sam. 25)' 01/02/16, https://paa.moore.edu.au/resource-center/ Last accessed May 2021

14   Sumner, *Men and Women in the Church*, p. 170

about authority, but because it makes us so vulnerable. We value autonomy and independence highly. Arianna Grande proclaimed on Instagram, 'I ... do not. belong. to anyone. but myself. and neither do you'.[15] She is right in as much as we are never 'owned' by others. A wife is never described as a man's property in the Bible. But Paul asks wives to yield to their husbands willingly and to give up their autonomy voluntarily. This is scary, but remember she is to do this in response to her husband's sacrificial love.

THE HUSBAND

If we think the wife's calling is hard, her husband faces an even more challenging task. He is called to love his wife as Christ loved the church, by giving himself up for her, and to care for her like his own body. This is not about taking control or having power or being the boss. It is not about ownership or making decisions. It is about giving up self-interest and living for the sake of another. It is a call to radical self-sacrifice, as Sumner says:

> *Self-sacrifice, by definition, must be enacted by the self. When Jesus laid down his life, he made it clear that no one could force him to die (John 10:18). He died voluntarily. He was crucified voluntarily. He laid down his life voluntarily. So the godly husband lays down his life voluntarily for his bride.*[16]

---

15 https://www.nytimes.com/2017/05/23/arts/music/what-ariana-grande-represents-to-her-fans.html Last accessed May 2021

16 Sumner, *Men and Women in the Church*, p. 170

Sadly, the church has frequently focused its teaching on wives and their role rather than the husband's calling. Women have been told to give up everything for their husbands, but husbands have not been taught that they are called to do the same. But many couples have discovered these truths for themselves and lived accordingly. I have seen marriages where husbands have shown extraordinary love, sacrificing their career prospects to care for their wives. I know of men who gave up their ambitions for the sake of their wives. It is a beautiful thing to see. God's plan for marriage, when fully embraced, does not diminish either partner but exalts them both, Sumner concludes:

> *The husband and wife participate together in a dynamic upward spiral of lifting each other up instead of putting each other down. They don't engage in battle with each other. For example, the husband does not say, 'down woman, I'm the boss!' Nor does the wife rebel against her husband. Instead, she lifts him up. He, in turn, lifts her up as well. As a result, they go up, up, up, up rather than down, down, down. There is no power struggle.*[17]

Rather than marriage being the source of oppression, God desires the reverse. Anne Bradstreet celebrated such an alliance in her poem:

> *To My Dear and Loving Husband*
> *If ever two were one, then surely we.*
> *If ever man were loved by wife, then thee;*
> *If ever wife was happy in a man,*

---

17   ibid. p. 171

Compare with me, ye women, if you can.
I prize thy love more than whole mines of gold
Or all the riches that the East doth hold.
My love is such that rivers cannot quench,
Nor ought but love from thee give recompense.
Thy love is such I can no way repay.
The heavens reward thee manifold, I pray.
Then while we live, in love let's so persevere
That when we live no more, we may live ever.
Anne Bradstreet (1678)

I know that this is not the experience in all marriages, but there are marriages in which this is being worked out (not perfectly because none of us are capable of such selfless love all the time). I can personally testify to having a husband who has enabled me to thrive – for which I am continually thankful. God's design for marriage is not one of control and ownership but a relationship for the mutual good of the other.

This is true in the sexual expression of marriage too. Paul explained it like this to the Corinthian church:

Since sexual immorality is occurring, each man should have sexual relations with his own wife, and each woman with her own husband. The husband should fulfil his marital duty to his wife, and likewise the wife to her husband. The wife does not have authority over her own body but yields it to her husband. In the same way, the husband does not have authority over his own body but yields it to his wife. Do not deprive each other except perhaps by mutual consent and for a time, so that you may devote yourselves to prayer. Then come together again so that Satan will not tempt you because of your lack of self-control.[18]

The expression of sexuality in marriage is an act of yielding to the other. Elena Ferrante described marital rape in her Neapolitan novel, *The Story of a New Name*. Lila was 'violated at his pleasure solely because now she belonged to him'.[19] In the UK, it wasn't until 1984 that rape in marriage was acknowledged as an offence; the idea had been that the wife does not have authority over her own body. But Paul, back in the first century, said this was wrong. The sexual act is one of voluntarily yielding to the other. It is not about coercion. No partner owns the other. Both partners are to provide for the other's sexual needs. Men and women are equal in the marriage bed. This is radical stuff. Paul acknowledges women's sexual needs as well as men's. Sex, according to the Bible, is about willingly giving to the other, and mutual consent.

THE MEANING OF MARRIAGE

Paul's teaching about marriage was not invented in a vacuum. He understood the theological meaning of marriage: marriage points to Christ's love for the church. We saw this picture in the last chapter: just as Hosea sacrificially loved his runaway bride, Christ gave Himself up for us. Biblical marriage is not an institution that makes women suffer under the weight of a domineering husband. A good marriage points to the way God loves His people.

---

18   1 Corinthians 7:2-5
19   Ferrante, *The Story of a New Name*

Of course, no marriage gets close to the love God has for His bride. God is a husband like no other. His love is extraordinary. As we saw earlier, most betrayed husbands do not forgive their wives but this husband, even after being hated, rescues and transforms His bride! He is the outstanding husband of the Bible. The rescue God won was not cheap, it involved His son dying on a cross, but through that death, He was able to betroth His bride to Him in perfect righteousness and justice, love and compassion.[20]

It is no wonder husbands are pointed to Him as the ultimate example. Christ is our bridegroom, the one who gave Himself up for us to make us holy and present us without stain or wrinkle or any other blemish. God's people look forward to the day when we will be united with Him. Brides take ages to get ready and don't usually see the bridegroom before the ceremony, but God's people are prepared by the bridegroom. The Bible finishes with this image:

> *Then I saw 'a new heaven and a new earth,' for the first heaven and the first earth had passed away, and there was no longer any sea. I saw the Holy City, the new Jerusalem, coming down out of heaven from God, prepared as a bride beautifully dressed for her husband. And I heard a loud voice from the throne saying, 'Look! God's dwelling-place is now among the people, and he will dwell with them. They will be his people, and God himself will be with them and be their God. "He will wipe every tear from their eyes. There will be no more death" or mourning or crying or pain, for the old order of things has passed away.'[21]*

20   Hosea 2:16-23

21   Revelation 21:1-4

In our fallen world marriage is marred. Feminists are right when they see the problems, but not all marriages are as bad as Simone de Beauvoir feared. Marriage can be good, although not perfect. Because of the fall, every good thing that God gave to us in Eden is tainted, bad or downright ugly; nothing is neutral. Some marriages have been very ugly, but others a joy. All marriages experience both good and bad times. We do not have perfect relationships, but in a good marriage, we get a tiny glimpse of God's extraordinary abundant, extravagant, absolute and perfect love. God is not a husband who fails us. Ed Shaw, a single pastor in Bristol, put it like this: marriage reveals the substance of the gospel and singleness reveals the sufficiency of the gospel. We don't need to be married to be fulfilled; we need the gospel. We learn about God's love through the imagery of marriage.

Do you know this love? Are you afraid that you have let God down too many times? He doesn't give up on us. He loves us more than any husband has ever loved a wife – quite a thought. He knows our inmost hearts, He knows our worst rebellions, our darkest secrets, our deepest pains, but He still woos us. He is calling to us tenderly. Remember those words from Hosea?

> *Therefore I am now going to allure her;*
> *I will lead her into the wilderness*
> *and speak tenderly to her.* [22]

---

22   Hosea 2:14

Do you fear that somehow you are excluded from a relationship with God? God is making those who weren't His people His beautiful bride:

I will plant her for myself in the land;
I will show my love to the one I called 'Not my loved one'.
I will say to those called 'Not my people', 'You are my people';
and they will say, 'You are my God.'[23]

We can be sure of this love. Look to Jesus. He gave Himself up for us by His death on the cross. This love is the most extravagant in the world. It is only in this love that we genuinely flourish whether we are married or not.

For Further Thought and Conversation
- What do you think the purpose of marriage is?
- What dangers are there in looking to a human relationship for fulfilment?
- What would make you feel fulfilled in life?

Read Hosea 2:16-23 and Revelation 21-22:5
- What is God promising His people?
- In what ways does this remind you of Eden (Genesis 2)?
- How do you feel about this picture?
- Do you share this hope for the future?

---

23   Hosea 2:23

12. LIBERATION

Imagine if Anne Bradstreet, Margaret Cavendish, Mary Wollstonecraft, Jane Austen, Marion Read, Elisabeth Cady Stanton and Simone de Beauvoir could come and cast an eye on modern Britain. Picture them walking onto a university campus and seeing women studying alongside men in the fields of medicine, law, architecture and engineering. Follow them as they visit the Houses of Parliament and listen to women ministers debate on the floor of the Commons. Watch their reactions to hearing political commentary from female journalists. As they leave Westminster, they will be aghast at women commuting to work, travelling unchaperoned and then amazed when they realise women are driving some of those trains and buses.

There has been a revolution. In 1998 *TIME Magazine* ran the cover: 'Is feminism dead?' A fair question at the end of the twentieth century in which women's status in law was made equal to that of men. It looked as though feminism was completed; girls could aim for anything. Dare I say our legal system had caught up with the Bible? I hope by now, you can see why I think that. The Bible is not sexist: it is remarkable. God offers women and men more than we can imagine. And we need what He offers.

Women's lives have been transformed, but this world is still broken. The effects of the fall remain this side of God's new creation. We experience them differently from previous generations, but their impact is the same. Germaine Greer, the unapologetic, unpopular, outspoken feminist observed at the turn of the millennium:

> *The millennial feminist has to be aware that oppression exerts itself in and through her most intimate relationships, beginning with the most intimate, her relationship with her body. More and more of her waking hours are to be spent in disciplining the recalcitrant body, fending off the diseases that it is heir to and making up for its inadequacies in shape, size, weight, colouring, hair distribution, muscle tone — and its incorrigible propensity for ageing. More of her life is wasted cleaning things that are already clean, trying to feed people who aren't hungry, and labouring to, in, from and for chain stores. Too much of her energy is sapped by being made to be afraid of everything but her real enemy, fear itself. She spends too much time waiting for things that will not happen, hoping for support and reinforcement that are withheld, apologising for matters beyond her control, longing for closeness to the ones she loves and being reconciled to distance.[1]*

Greer identified the longing we all have to be satisfied. There are many problems feminism cannot solve. However much

---

1   Germaine Greer, *The Whole Woman* (Doubleday, 1999)

freedom women gain; we are still trapped in our fallenness. We experience the brokenness of this world.

Sweden is a country that has embraced equality, social reforms, and prides itself on its policies to help work-life balance. However, the rates of chronic stress-related illness or 'burnout' have rapidly increased. Among 25–29-year-olds, there has been a 144 per cent rise in workers off sick with exhaustion. This rate is higher among women. Professor Marie Asberg explains:

> *The brain cannot differentiate between employment and other work-like tasks, such as planning a lot of activities in your spare time, having a competitive hobby, or staying up late to ensure your social media profile is up-to-date… the brain doesn't care if you get paid for it, or not. Most people who hit the wall are very ambitious and don't sleep enough. They want to succeed and show the world how good they are, so they overtax their own strengths and endurance.*[2]

The social pressure to be fit, to look good, to use your time well, to be involved in political activism, to create the perfect home, to post about 'living your best life' and have a successful career is overwhelming. Our culture sucks us dry. It promises satisfaction, but it is a relentless pursuit. We need to stop.

Restoring our relationship with God is our most fundamental need. This is a lesson that Christabel Pankhurst learnt. Christabel, along with her mother Emmeline and her sisters, was a leader of the suffrage movement in Britain. Her

---

2   https://www.bbc.com/worklife/article/20190719-why-is-burnout-rising-in-the-land-of-work-life-balance Last accessed August 2019

early years were taken up in militant activism. She was arrested frequently and conducted hunger strikes. However, in the second half of her life, she came to a realisation: 'she was trying to build a human-made utopia, an impossible achievement. She came to faith in Christ and joined the Plymouth Brethren.'[3] She spent her last years lecturing in America as a former suffragist revolutionary and an evangelical Christian. She knew to campaign for women was important and gave most of her life to it, but she realised there is more to this life than this world and that the ultimate liberation and freedom everyone needs are found in God alone.

Jesus once met two women. He went to their home with His disciples. Mary spent every moment she could listening to Jesus' teaching. She sat alongside the men and absorbed it all. Her sister, Martha, was trying to get dinner ready. She had a house full of guests and was overwhelmed by the work that needed doing. I can relate to that. It is annoying when there is lots to do, and those you expect to help are sitting around doing nothing. Martha was irritated and complained to Jesus. Her cause was just, and she was sure that He would take her side; after all, wasn't Mary failing in her domestic responsibilities and duties? Instead, Jesus said this:

> 'Martha, Martha,' the Lord answered, 'you are worried and upset about many things, but few things are needed – or indeed only one. Mary has chosen what is better, and it will not be taken away from her.'[4]

---

3   Diana Lynn Severance, *Feminine Threads: Women in the Tapestry of History* (Christian Focus, 2011), p. 291

4   Luke 10:41-42

Mary had made a better choice. It was better to listen to Jesus than provide for her guests. Jesus placed the need for a woman to learn from Him way above her fulfilling her traditional responsibilities. Even though it meant dinner would not be made!

There will always be a lot to do. Demands on our time are endless. But to let those responsibilities stop us from listening to Jesus is a tragedy. We need to be still and know that God is God. We need to stop and listen to Him. The burden of the millennial woman is exhausting. Work is continuous: meals always need preparing, housework is never finished, the garden (if we have one) is perpetual toil. When we have time to rest, we feel compelled to keep going to get everything perfect. Pursuing materialism is like spiralling down a never-ending rabbit hole. We want to be admired, praised, or at the very least, accepted. We become enslaved by the beautiful things that God has given us. Our friendships and families are both a delight and a burden. We are tired. We have brief moments of rest, but we fail to see that what we need is to sit at Jesus' feet. We need His life-giving refreshment. Jesus offers that to us. He calls us to come:

> *Come to me, all you who are weary and burdened, and I will give you rest. Take my yoke upon you and learn from me, for I am gentle and humble in heart, and you will find rest for your souls. For my yoke is easy, and my burden is light.*[5]

Jesus offers us more than anything our world can offer. Don't get me wrong. I am not saying come to Jesus, and you will

---

5   Matthew 11:28-30

be permanently happy, satisfied and without any difficulties. In previous chapters we have seen God's people face suffering and hardship. This side of heaven creation is groaning, longing for the day when everything is restored. Rest doesn't mean not doing anything. Coming to Jesus involves change. It means learning from Him and following Him; submitting to Jesus as our master turns our lives upside down. Responding to Jesus' call will mean giving up our independence and living with Him as Lord. That may sound scary, but Jesus is not a master who abuses His servants. He made Himself nothing, taking the form of a servant for our sake. He is not a master who looks down on His servants; instead, He calls us friends. He is not a master who has no patience with our failings; instead, He was tempted in every way and offers us mercy and grace in our time of need. He understands. We can take His yoke. We can learn from Him. He has been there before us. He is with us every step of the way, and He is leading us home. Jesus is the only one who can give us rest but He was clear that following Him involves a cost.

> *Whoever wants to be my disciple must deny themselves and take up their cross and follow me. For whoever wants to save their life will lose it, but whoever loses their life for me and for the gospel will save it.*[6]

The apostle Peter knew this cost first-hand and later wrote to Christians who were facing severe persecution:

---

6   Mark 8:34-35

Dear friends, do not be surprised at the fiery ordeal that has come on you to test you, as though something strange were happening to you. But rejoice inasmuch as you participate in the sufferings of Christ, so that you may be overjoyed when his glory is revealed.[7]

Peter knew that taking up the cross was tough, but worth it. The New Testament contains the names of many other disciples who experienced this reality. Among them are many women, who came to Christ and whose lives were turned upside down. Women like the businesswomen Lydia,[8] who opened up her home for believers in a city hostile to the church. Phoebe, who supported many people including Paul and was entrusted with arguably one of the most important letters of the New Testament, to take to Rome.[9] Priscilla who, along with her husband, risked her life for Paul and taught one of the foremost leaders of the early church.[10] There are others who we are told worked hard for the Lord. They did not live comfortable lives, but they knew the truth of the gospel of Jesus. They looked forward to their heavenly rest and could testify to knowing a peace that passes all understanding.

We fear following Christ will mean getting less from life. Eve fell for that trick. She thought God wanted to diminish her and that stolen fruit would offer her more, although it turned out to be poison. But God wants to give us more, not less. Don't be seduced by the voice of folly:

---

7   1 Peter 4:12-13

8   Acts 16:13-15, 40

9   Romans 16:1-2

10   Romans 16:3, Acts 18:24-28

'Stolen water is sweet;
food eaten in secret is delicious!'
But little do they know that the dead are there,
that her guests are deep in the realm of the dead.[11]

Folly tries to seduce us, but it offers nothing but death. Wisdom provides us with so much more:

Wisdom has built her house;
she has set up its seven pillars.
She has prepared her meat and mixed her wine;
she has also set her table.
She has sent out her servants, and she calls
from the highest point of the city,
'Let all who are simple come to my house!'
To those who have no sense she says,
'Come, eat my food
and drink the wine I have mixed.
Leave your simple ways and you will live;
walk in the way of insight.'[12]

There is a banquet on offer. God offers us more than our wildest dreams and imaginings. It is on offer for women as well as men. Don't listen to the lies that say otherwise. Life without God does not satisfy. It leads to much less. Choose what is better, and it will not be taken away from you:

---

11   Proverbs 9:17-18

12   Proverbs 9:1-6

Liberation

The Spirit and the Bride say, 'Come!' And let the one who hears say, 'Come!' Let the one who is thirsty come; and let the one who wishes take the free gift of the water of life.[13]

FOR FURTHER THOUGHT AND CONVERSATION

- What burdens people today?
- What do we think we need to fulfil us?
- How do you understand rest?
- Imagine a world that is not fallen, what would it look like?

READ MARK 8:27-38

- How can you be still and listen to Jesus?
- Do you believe following Jesus offers more than living life without Him?
- What will it mean for you to follow Jesus?
- What will be your next step?

---

13   Revelation 22:17

Also available from Christian Focus Publications...

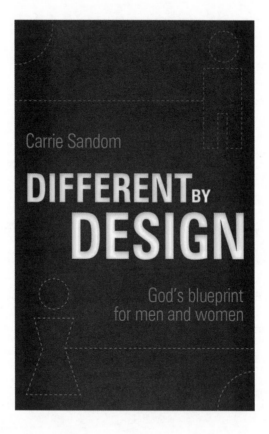

Carrie Sandom

DIFFERENT BY
DESIGN

God's blueprint
for men and women

978-1-8455-0782-4

Different by Design

God's blueprint for men and women

Carrie Sandom

Men and women are created in the image of God to reflect God's own nature and being to reflect the perfect equality, diversity, and unity of the Trinity. Carrie Sandom presents the Biblical view of gender roles for marriage, the church, and the workplace, and shows how they fit into a modern context.

Different by Design *is an impressive outline of the Bible's teaching on the sensitive subject of gender. Carrie's faithful handling of the Biblical text and its application today combines depth and clarity with simplicity and grace. She argues convincingly that the differences between men and women go much deeper than the biological and, far from being oppressive, the complementary nature of their relationship is part of God's loving design for human flourishing.*

Vaughan Roberts
Rector of St Ebbe's, Oxford and Director of Proclamation Trust

Throughout the book, Carrie gives practical encouragements to live out our God-given roles, particularly in our families and churches, liberating us to be who God created us to be and inspiring us to do the work he created us to do. Males and females, whether single or married, will benefit from reading this book. May it help women, in particular, see the beauty and wisdom of God's design for our lives.

Keri Folmar
Author & Pastor's Wife from Dubai

Diana Lynn Severance

MARY BLANDINA
MARCELLA ETHELBERGA
MARGARET DELETT CALVIN
ANNE BOLEYN ELIZABETH
ANNE HUTCHINSON
SARAH FLORENCE
DOREEN NIGHTINGALE
BOOTH
JONI
EARECKSON
ADA

Feminine
Threads

Women in the Tapestry of Christian History

978-1-8455-0640-7

Feminine Threads

Women in the Tapestry of Christian History

Diana Lynn Severance

From commoner to queen, the women in this book embraced the freedom and the power of the Gospel in making their unique contributions to the unfolding of history. Wherever possible, the women here speak for themselves, from their letters, diaries or published works. The true story of women in Christian history inspires, challenges and demonstrates the grace of God producing much fruit throughout time.

Feminine Threads *is a must-read for men and women alike, but especially so for young women who need to have a clear view of the contributions that women before them have made to the Christian faith.*

Carolyn McCulley
Conference Speaker and Author of *Radical Womanhood: Feminine Faith in a Feminist World*

'What women these Christians have!' exclaimed Libanius, the fourth century teacher of rhetoric. His words are amply underscored and vividly illustrated in this deeply researched and highly readable survey of the last 2,000 years – an appraisal that Diana Severance invariably places against the enduring touchstone of Scripture.

Richard Bewes, OBE (1939 – 2019)
Formerly of All Souls Church, Langham Place, London, England

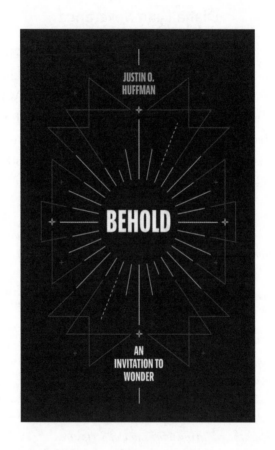

JUSTIN O.
HUFFMAN

BEHOLD

AN
INVITATION TO
WONDER

978-1-5271-0723-6

Behold

An Invitation to Wonder

Justin Huffman

We are starving for want of wonder. In what we perceive to be the desert wasteland of daily life and regular responsibilities, our souls hunger for more. We instinctively feel there must be more to life than merely waiting for the next big movie to be released, or the next sport season to come back around, or the next holiday to arrive on the calendar. We long to be truly in awe. Justin O. Huffman invites us to meditate on ten of the occasions the command 'Behold' is used in the New Testament, and to feast on the wonderful truth we find there.

... points to the all glorious and the awesome – to the wondrous person and work of Jesus Christ. Dear reader, as you read 'Behold' may your heart be wonderstruck at the glories of who Christ is and what He has done.

Christina Fox
Counselor, retreat speaker and author

Justin Huffman takes the familiar truths of Christ's gospel and helps us to view them again with wonder—a sense of glory that both fascinates us and fills us with awe. Here is a book that focuses attention on Jesus and says, 'Behold your God!'

Joel R. Beeke
President, Puritan Reformed Theological Seminary, Grand Rapids, Michigan

100 Devotional Readings
on Union With Christ

HOW TO LIVE AN
'IN CHRIST' LIFE

KENNETH BERDING

978-1-5271-0559-1

How to Live an 'In Christ' Life

100 Devotional Readings on Union with Christ

Kenneth Berding

Everywhere we look in the letters of Paul we encounter 'in Christ.' But how many of us know why the Apostle Paul uses this expression—or ones like it—over and over again in his letters? What is so important about being in Christ? Is it possible that when Paul talks about inChristness, he is handing us a set of keys that will open up his letters and reveal what is most essential to living the Christian life? In these 100 devotional readings, we discover why inChristness is so important and how to live an in-Christ life.

Understanding the meaning and significance of our new identity as believers in relationship to Jesus Christ is the number one concern of the Apostle Paul in his letters. Deep prayerful reflection on these key elements of life in Christ will transform you from the inside out.

Clinton E. Arnold
Dean and Professor of New Testament, Talbot School of Theology
(Biola University), La Mirada, California

I cannot remember the last time I read a book on union with Christ and was so convicted that I stopped and prayed. Without compromising biblical and theological depth, Berding unveils the innumerable ways union with Christ makes a real difference in the Christian life.

Matthew Barrett
Associate Professor of Christian Theology, Midwestern Baptist
Theological Seminary, Kansas City, Missouri

Christian Focus Publications

Our mission statement —

STAYING FAITHFUL

In dependence upon God we seek to impact the world
through literature faithful to His infallible Word, the Bible.
Our aim is to ensure that the Lord Jesus Christ is presented as
the only hope to obtain forgiveness of sin, live a useful life and
look forward to heaven with Him.

Our books are published in four imprints:

CHRISTIAN
FOCUS

Popular works including biographies, commentaries, basic doctrine
and Christian living.

CHRISTIAN
HERITAGE

Books representing some of the
best material from the rich heritage
of the church.

MENTOR

Books written at a level suitable
for Bible College and seminary
students, pastors, and other serious
readers. The imprint includes
commentaries, doctrinal studies,
examination of current issues and
church history.

CF4•K

Children's books for quality Bible
teaching and for all age groups: Sunday
school curriculum, puzzle and activity
books; personal and family devotional
titles, biographies and inspirational stories — because you are never too young
to know Jesus!

Christian Focus Publications Ltd,
Geanies House, Fearn, Ross-shire,
IV20 1TW, Scotland, United Kingdom.
www.christianfocus.com